KAMLOOPS TAPESTRY

An Anthology put together by the Interior Authors Group of Kamloops, and written by members of the IAG

Kamloops Tapestry

With stories and poems by:
- Lori Marks
- June Powell
- Allen Hern
- Alex McGilvery
- Janet Miller
- Corea Ladner
- Elma Schemenauer
- Eleanor Hancock
- Rita Joan Dozlaw
- Ward Pycock
- Dana Ramstedt
- Eileen Bell
- Jan Petrar

All copyrights belong to the authors, 2020

ISN978-1-989092-38-5

Published by the Interior Authors Group through Celticfrog Publishing

ACKNOWLEDGEMENTS

The members of the Collected Works Committee were
Dana Ramstedt, Chair
Eileen Bell
Karen Ramstedt
Alex McGilvery
Blazej Szpakowicz

Editors
Alex McGilvery
Blazej Szpakowicz

Formatting and Cover Design
Alex McGilvery

Proofreaders
Eileen Bell
June Powell
Dana Ramstedt

Photo Credit for Cover
Karen Ramstedt

Thanks to the Kamloops Museum and Archives for allowing us to use photos from their collection

TABLE OF CONTENTS

A Higher Perspective on Battle Bluff	1
Love Life	8
Lori Ann Mark	
The Wanda Sue	10
Onstage Bloopers	15
June Carter Powell	
Ahhh - Kamloops	21
Allen Hern	
Tranquille Dark	27
Alex McGilvery	
Kamloops	34
Janet Miller	
Kamloops? Seriously?	36
Corea Ladner	
Returning To Kamloops.	43
Gold And Roses	50
Elma (Martens) Schemenauer	
Photos From the Archives	55
Kamloops Museum and Archives	
What The Crows Say	62
Eleanor Hancock	
A Portrait Of Precocious	69
Peace O' Mind	71
Lady Thompson	73
Introducing: Suzette Roche	75
At The Sagebrush Theatre	
Rita Joan Dozlaw	

Dylan's Day	82
Ward Pycock	
Who Am I	89
Hammock At Sunset	91
I Got Blocks!	93
Stresses Ease	98
Dana Ramstedt	
From Selkirk To Sagebrush	101
Eileen Bell	
Where Am I?	114
Jan Petrar	

Lori Ann Mark

A HIGHER PERSPECTIVE
ON BATTLE BLUFF

By Lori Ann Mark

Moving back to Kamloops after being gone for almost two decades was difficult. I'd never imagined returning, as it represented tremendous loss and pain; nevertheless, here I was. Even though I was happy to be closer to my kids, my first few months in Kamloops were dismal; I grieved for my old life, managed unpleasant memories that surfaced upon moving back and struggled to settle enough to call Kamloops my home.

Being a person who values and pursues personal growth, I had to do something to change my state of mind, so I decided to go hiking. A great activity for processing thoughts and getting the creative juices flowing. Unsure of where to go, I pulled out my phone and searched for a hiking spot close to home and not too intimidating. Battle Bluff fit the bill. Finding no one to go with me, I chose to go and explore on my own.

The following Saturday, I loaded my knapsack holding myself accountable to my commitment to tackle the notorious Battle Bluff. I was impressed with the positive reviews and intrigued by the battle history, having gone through battles of my own. I was unsure of what to do about the memories that were threatening

the peace and growth I had worked so hard to achieve. Determined to get out of my funk, I headed out to follow unknown paths and find some answers.

I was excited to begin my little adventure with my pack on my back. It had been a while since I had hiked, and I had never ventured out alone into the wilderness.

Just a few steps into the ravine, I saw a sign warning of cougars in the area. Remembering the cars in the parking area, I knew that there were other hikers out there, so I swallowed my fear and pressed on.

Jutting out here and there were random rocks and roots which caused me to slow down and navigate carefully through the narrow, tree-lined canyon Even while watching my step I stopped several times to look around and spotted many interesting things, including an old, smashed-up truck, which made me wonder how in the world it had got there in the first place. There were sandy hills and a rock cliff, a perfect spot for a cougar to perch. Trees bereft of life, strewn all over the hillsides for no apparent reason, reminded me of my childhood games, Kerplunk and Pick-up Sticks.

While meandering through this Wild West setting, enjoying all there was to see, I kept a watchful eye out for any movement in the brush.

The trail brought me to the base of a small rounded hill, with the option to go left or right. Energized and brimming with curiosity I made my way along the well-worn path to the right. Around the bend I was rewarded with an incredibly stunning view. Anxious to see more, I climbed a small hill and took in the wide-open skies and the rolling hills with some tall, scraggly pines.

Scanning the rough terrain, I noticed how different it was in every direction. There were eroding sedimentary banks that looked like they contained some layers of harder volcanic rock, jagged cliffs with terrifying drop-offs and open grassy meadows. The area was mostly bare, with dry grasses spotted with sagebrush, and to my surprise, I saw a tidy row of telegraph poles. Completing this work of art were flashes of jewelled brilliance dancing across the large body of water below. I stood there intoxicated with sunshine and fresh mountain air. Satisfied, knowing I

Kamloops Tapestry

had chosen wisely, I returned to the path below me, eager to get up to the bluff.

After passing yet another rusted-out vehicle, a turquoise wagon; I headed toward the mountain, which many years before had earned itself the name Battle Bluff. I felt free of the anxiety I  had been experiencing. I felt alive again and each step forward affirmed I was there for a reason. Soon I heard people descending, which brought some comfort to me. I wasn't alone with the possibility of cougars or other predators. We passed each other on the narrow path and exchanged warm, knowing smiles, like we shared a secret, enjoying our love for the outdoors. I recall wondering on my ascent why I had waited so long to get out hiking. Note to self: don't stop doing what you love to do, especially when you are in a challenging situation.

The last part of my climb was steeper, the ground slightly more challenging to navigate, with moss-covered rock faces and steep, muddy trails. Winter was desperately trying to survive the quick arrival of spring. The small patches of ice in the shady areas among pines, boulders and rock crevices were easy to avoid. Thankfully, it was a short trek, because it had been a long

Lori Ann Mark

time since I had gone climbing and I felt overdressed for the unseasonably warm winter sun.

Upon arriving at the pinnacle, I was not disappointed.

The view surpassed my expectations. I took off my outer layer, pulled out my blanket and set it on a little nook between the rocks to sit and reflect on my journey.

So many thoughts flowed through my heart and mind. For years, I was convinced that change was hard, even impossible. The odds were against me. My experiences showed me it's easier to repeat the same behaviours and make the same choices almost against one's own will. The memories had caused a lot of hurt in the past. I expected to be overwhelmed recalling many difficult experiences. But surprisingly, I wasn't, instead I reveled in peace.

My life had once been steeped in the drama of my past, like a wet teabag staining everything it touched. Shame and embarrassment contributed to my shy disposition and I tucked away my memories in a drawer. Now it was time to open the drawer. I knew my life was different, but I wondered if the changes would be enough to carry me through. Perhaps that was why I was here.

Looking around, I saw nothing particularly beautiful about the barren land of nondescript grey dirt, shale and dried grass, but the entire view was a masterpiece. Over the years, the landscape had been bombarded by powerful storms, torrential rains, heat waves and droughts. Wind, snow and ice all impacted the layout of the land. This seemed like my life. In this place, my story seemed not as bleak as I had once believed. I allowed myself to remember some fond memories previously overshadowed by my own focus on negative events. I may not have chosen a lot of the things that happened, but who does? I can appreciate it, however, because it is all a part of what made me dig

down deep and find meaning and purpose in my life. We cannot change the events of our past, but we can rewrite the story with positive reflection. We can look at our past simply as what was and not have it define us. Motivational speaker and author Wayne Dyer said, "When you change the way you look at things, the things you look at change." I have found that to be true.

If you are in a battle, wanting to make some positive changes or go after a dream, first see clearly where you are and where you want to go so you can map it out. Anything worth having takes focus, effort and commitment. Fill your backpack with things that will motivate and sustain you on your journey. Enlist a friend, a mentor or a coach to help you find your way or keep you moving in the right direction. Every small step and positive choice counts. Be patient with yourself. It has taken years to develop the habits and lifestyle that you have. Writer and editor Dorothea Brande said, "habits are strong and jealous." That is what makes change difficult, and it's what makes it so rewarding.

Life will always provide us with challenges; you might as well go through them, benefiting from the process of growth. It's overcoming those challenges that yields wisdom, increased strength and positive momentum. Progress feels amazing and really increases our happiness factor.

I'm grateful for finding my way back to Kamloops, and I have found it to be a wonderful, supportive community. I'm enjoying getting out in nature at the many lakes and trails in the area. I love my life. It wasn't the city that was the problem, nor was it my past; it was my own thinking and the meaning I gave it. My perception changed even more positively the day I decided to hike Battle Bluff.

I have found my way home. Life is an exciting journey, which is very different for everyone. I hope to see you at the top!

LOVE LIFE

Love life
Keep it simple,
Expectant eyes, a smile, a dimple.
Kind and sweet, warm and bright,
Enjoy the sun and the moonlight.
Take the paintbrush in your hand,
Paint a picture, make it grand,
Colour it with gifts of love
Touching, loving, laughing, caring
You won't miss out if you're daring
Don't hide behind your failure's past
The grip it has will never last
Look ahead to what can be
Tear down the walls and you'll be free
You're not selfish for wanting more
Empty, aching, searching, needing to explore
The world we live in, the people we meet
Are part of what makes life so sweet,
But if you're down and wear a frown
Groping, moping, barely hoping
You'll miss out on the joy life holds
So, break the mold, be strong, be bold
With head held high no need to cry
You have love inside your heart
And that's exactly where to start
To love life.

Lori Ann Mark

Lori embraces life, love and personal growth. She believes it's never too late to dream and make incredible lasting change. In her late forties, she ran a half-marathon after losing 65lbs and then graduated from high school. In her early fifties she went river rafting, bungee jumping and discovered hiking. Her first love is her family, and she has recently become a very proud grandma. While working full time, she started a mobile life coaching business, makes time for ongoing education, writes, dabble in the arts, and enjoys multiple outdoor activities which mostly includes her new puppy Lucy.

The *Wanda Sue* with skipper Gunnar Slack.

THE WANDA SUE

By June Carter Powell.

For many years the *Wanda Sue* lent a romantic ambiance to the city of Kamloops as she cruised the Thompson Rivers. With two daily trips, an excellent menu and well-informed commentators, what better way to enjoy the fantastic scenery than to take a cruise on the *Wanda Sue?*

June Carter Powell

Her history is as intriguing as the craft herself. George Slack Sr. retired in 1976, but he didn't stop working. He was an amazing man with the energy of someone much younger than his sixty-five years. From his home overlooking the river, he watched the waves lash the shore, kingfishers dive for food and herons wait for unwary fish to scoop up, and the occasional motorboat. The mighty Thompson River was missing something.

There should have been a paddle wheeler chugging up and down that river. He had no experience as a shipbuilder, although he did have the keen mind of an engineer and was an avid reader. He would build one!

For the next seven years he worked each day in his own backyard. He was not a romantic man, but he did have a dream.

Its construction wasn't an easy task, nor was it without glitches and painful decisions. The *Wanda Sue* was built from bow to stern by George Slack alone. With hard work and dedication, his dream became a reality. The only help he had was from a family friend, Ed Gould, who was a crane operator. When it was fully constructed, Ed lifted the hull and placed it in the water.

The *Wanda Sue*'s maiden voyage was in 1983, as it began a twenty-year career chugging up and down the Thompson Rivers. The sturdy little craft was piloted by Gunnar Slack, George's son. When George passed away in 2003, he was happy that he had lived long enough to share his dream with many others.

We scheduled our daily dog walks so we could watch the drawbridge lift to allow the *Wanda Sue* to sail under the railway on her one o'clock voyages. There were always some tense moments as we waited for the bridge to rise, but that was half the fun. Who could resist going on a cruise after waving to passengers as it continued on its way?

Walking on the narrow wharf to embark on a cruise was an adventure all its own. Waves washed up nearly to our toes as we made our way to the gate. The wharf would bob in the water, making kids squeal with delight and their mothers hang on to them lest they go for an unplanned swim. A walk through the gate and up the steps, all the while being rocked back and forth, added to the adventure.

The swift current carried us to Rabbit Island easily, and then her powerful motors pushed against the strong waters and whirlpools of the mighty Thompson to return to home port.

Special family dinners were eaten in her dining room and many a wedding reception was celebrated on her deck.

As we slid into the twenty-first century, environmental concerns were raised about dredging the river to accommodate the need for deeper water. This brought to Kamloops the end of an era. The *Wanda Sue* spent a year running scenic tours from Salmon Arm but returned to Kamloops to retire.

She almost made a comeback in 2005, when the Kamloops Brandenburg Orchestra, directed by Cvetozar Vutev, planned to perform a July 1 concert on the paddle wheeler.

June Carter Powell

A group of willing workers swabbed the decks, cleaned the bathrooms and vacuumed the dining room, giving passengers opportunity to experience the paddle wheeler one more time. There were some anxious moments when the window cleaners stood on the narrow ledge over the churning water, but miraculously, no one fell overboard.

Although the *Wanda Sue* was still seaworthy, the plan was abandoned because the high cost of insurance needed to carry musical instruments was prohibitive.

While a concert was played aboard the royal barge on the River Thames in honour of King George the First, ours was on the banks of the Thompson River. The king was portrayed by singer Bill Brown, with Christo Vutev as the narrator and his brother Ivan as the king's page. Members of the Kamloops Brandenburg Orchestra dressed in eighteenth-century costumes performed Handel's *Water Music* and *Music for the Royal Fireworks*, written specially for the king. Many a musician peered over his shoulder to steal a look at the fireworks.

As the sun dipped below the horizon the romantic evening was brought to a close.

Today the *Wanda Sue* is docked on Thompson Ave. in Valleyview, a reminder that not so long ago, the picturesque paddle wheeler, the dream of George Slack Sr., travelled the Thompson Rivers.

The builder's grandson, George Slack Jr., says, "Grandfather Slack built two smaller-scale sternwheelers after the *Wanda Sue*. He constructed the *Slackwater*, then he bought a large lifeboat off a cruise ship and decked it in. He built a cabin, installed a motor

Kamloops Tapestry

recycled from a Mercedes Diesel and named her the *Goldie-Jean*."

Information supplied by George Slack Jr.

The Kamloops Brandenburg Orchestra performs three concerts per year, including one yearly concert, while dressed in eighteenth-century costumes reminiscent of those worn in 1717 on the Thames. Of special mention are Annette Dominic, Katharine Shewchuk and Rhiannon Nachbaur, who made many of the costumes, and Irene Whitfield, first Concert Master.

June Powell

ONSTAGE BLOOPERS

Nothing that happens onstage is unrehearsed. Anyone who has ever played in an orchestra, engaged in stand-up comedy, or competed in a festival or sports event, knows the rules. Never share your concerns with the audience. Recover as quickly as possible and carry on.

It is only with practiced stage presence that any performer can pass off the little bloopers that occur as part of the show. Occasionally even that doesn't work, and the audience enjoys the glitches too. This is where stage personality takes over.

Here are a few glaring errors that were too good to be kept a secret.

Names used with permission.

***

School Band directors know all about unexpected happenings first-hand. Don Bennett shared this one with me.

Before he directed his first school band concert of the year, he had trained his young students to never show their feelings during a performance and to play with confidence. Above all, enjoy the music and the audience.

He raised his baton with a flair, making a wide arc to give the downbeat. With a percussive crash, his baton caught the edge of a boy's music stand, scattering the pages onto the floor.

"What did I do?" the boy asked in dismay.

Kamloops Tapestry

"Nothing," Don said. "It was all my fault." He got down on his knees and helped the student pick up his music and replace the pages on the stand in the proper order. Someone in the audience began to applaud and everyone followed, so he and the student stood to acknowledge their appreciation.

Don said it set the mood for the rest of the concert, which was a successful performance.

***

Here's a couple of music mix-ups that happen more often than you imagine.

New to the music scene, Joe Joslin's first concert could have been a traumatic affair. At the ripe old age of fifty-two he first picked up a viola, learned the strange new clef, and discovered firsthand that it wasn't all fun and games. Faced with an audience for the first time, he tried to look relaxed.

He placed the first piece on his stand, lifted the instrument to his chin, and played with confidence and bravado. Hey, this was fun!

The next piece didn't go quite as planned, but without losing his cool, he continued co-ordinating his bow strokes with the rest of the ensemble. This was a feat in itself. He was playing *The Kentucky Waltz* in 3/4 time in the key of F while everyone else played the hoedown, *Soldier's Joy* in 4/4 time in the key of G.

It all goes to show that nothing is impossible. With his stage personality intact, he stood to acknowledge the applause, smiling broadly.

***

June Powell

Mike Powell is an old hand at playing for an audience. He has played for years in every group in Kamloops, often rushing home from work to grab a bite to eat on the run, to dash out to yet another rehearsal, and another concert.

Weddings require split second timing, and complete concentration. The quartet was in tune, the bride beautiful and the groom handsome. *Pachelbel's Canon* was well played, and Mike smiled with confidence. The church was filled to capacity with guests who had seen him play on many stages.

The second piece, Nat King Cole's *Unforgettable* posed some problems. The first four measures fit perfectly but then he struggled to coordinate the notes, and actually stopped playing. The second-violin player leaned over to see his music and whispered, "You're playing the wrong piece."

In a jiffy Mike put the right music on his stand and continued playing as if nothing had happened. Did anyone notice? No, they were watching the lovely bride.

***

When Kamloops Symphony was very young, we had three guest conductors for one season. *The New World Symphony* by Anton Dvorak was a good choice. The beginning was beautiful but when the mood changed to the serene English horn solo, the player and director had different opinions as to tempo. Neither one would give in, so it became a battle of wits to determine who would win.

Time dragged on as we tried to stay focused. It was evident that not only were the community players lost but so was the director. The soloist was still doing his own thing while the orchestra members were unsure who they should follow.

Some of us played only the chord notes, dragging our feet until at last we spied a player who looked confident. Like a flock of lost sheep, we fell in time with him. The soloist played the final note and the director found his place. *The New World Symphony* ended as it had begun, with professional finesse.

***

Before Kamloops had an orchestra, Lilian, Jose and Lore played with the Okanagan Symphony, making weekly trips to Kelowna. On one memorable winter afternoon, the road had patches of black ice and their car slipped into a ditch. It was getting dark and they still hadn't been successful in shovelling their way out. Finally, a car stopped, and two rather uncouth gentlemen offered to help. They pushed and pulled and finally drove the car back onto the road. They refused money, but when they discovered that Lilian, Jose and Lore were musicians on their way to play a concert in Kelowna, they had one request. Would the ladies tune their guitars before they left? Of course, they would, and they did.

"Good luck," the gentlemen said as they waved goodbye. "Say hello to your friends!"

The musicians arrived in Kelowna as the stage manager gave the last call to go onstage. Dashing into a washroom to change into her formal gown, Lilian was horrified to see the hem of her dress swirling in the toilet. Undaunted, she sloshed cold water on it, blotted it hastily with paper towels and sailed onstage as regally as Queen Victoria. As it dried, it took on a strange odour, so she sloshed more water on it at the intermission.

The story quickly circulated throughout the orchestra, but the audience was unaware of the drama taking place onstage.

***

Last on the list is a true story written at my own expense.

I was seventeen years old and had a walk-on speaking role in a play, *The Bishop's Candlesticks*. All I had to say was one line of four words.

The scene was set, and I entered centre stage with a great deal of confidence, having worked diligently to make my voice project. The words were straightforward. There was no room for error. "Hark! A pistol shot!" was about the easiest line to remember. What could possibly go wrong?

However, in a well-rehearsed stage voice, I blurted out "Hark, a postil s***!"

The shocked silence that followed lasted for only seconds before the entire audience cracked up. The laughter carried over into the bleachers and got louder and louder until the applause finally died out. A few giggles could still be heard as it faded away.

Some mistakes are simply unfixable and there is nothing one can do about them but take a bow.

Kamloops Tapestry

June Carter Powell lives in Kamloops with one husband, Michael, and two cats, Francie and Smoker. Although an octogenarian, she plays the viola in *Kamloops Brandenburg Orchestra* and in *The Thompson Valley Orchestra* as well as *Ordinary People*.

Her mother always said she embellished most stories to make them more interesting, so June thought she should use this talent somewhere. Creative writing!

Published works include *Under the Blue Wig*, *The Second Ending* and short stories in *Grandmothers' Necklace*, and several IAG publications, *Collected Works, Away From Home, Blue River, Dark Waters* and *Kaleidoscope*.

Allen Hern

AHHH - KAMLOOPS

By Allen Hern

Almost there! In the summer heat of June 1977, our green van was following a U-Haul truck on the last leg of the long journey from Sudbury, Ontario, to Kamloops, British Columbia.

2,267 miles (3,648 kilometers) lay behind us, and we were getting excited as we neared our destination. Past Chase, along the South Thompson River, past the Lafarge Cement plant, we counted down the miles. Now we were drawing near to the Dallas the community on the east end of Kamloops, and the trailer park which was to be our temporary home.

"Are we there yet?" was the question on the lips of nine-year-old Juanita, and seven-year-old Ian. Perhaps three-and-a-half year old Darryl was not yet asking the question, but he certainly was caught up in the expectations of his brother and sister, his mother Sheila, and me. We were all looking forward to getting out of the vehicle.

Suddenly a shredded trailer tire caused the trailer to swerve, and we made a hasty pull-off to the side of the road. By going very slowly, we were able to cover the last miles to our destination.

That was the second mishap we experienced on the long journey. 'Adventures in Moving:' was that not the slogan for U-Haul at that time?

It was with a deep sigh of contentment, and prayers of thanksgiving that the seven of us stepped out of our vehicle and the moving truck and found our way into the trailer which would be our lodging place for the next six months.

Our first challenge was to find a home.

We found a lot at the corner of Dallas Drive and Barnhartvale Road - "the first home you can reach in Dallas."

By Christmas our contractor had completed our new dwelling. Those who have had the experience know how glad Sheila and I were to empty out the storage spaces in various homes to bring everything to our new abode.

The kids settled into Dallas Elementary School, enjoying the opportunity after school and on the weekends to ride their bikes around the area with their friends.

Could it be that in those years, from 1977 to 1986, we didn't have to walk the kids to school each day or worry about where they and their friends were playing? Have things really changed that much? Yes, they have, to our sorrow.

We had come to Kamloops to give leadership to a new church. Dallas Barnhartvale Baptist was started as a daughter work of First Baptist Church on Columbia Street. They gave away wonderful families to get this new work started, then repeated the process within a short time, in starting Westsyde Baptist Church.

For four and a half years, our slowly growing church family met in the library of the R.L. Clemitson Public School in Barnhartvale. Sunday by Sunday, the folks prepared for a church service and Sunday School among the stacks in those rather crowded quarters.

Allen Hern

At last the city gave permission to set the bulldozers to work pushing the top off one of the clay hills just up Todd Road. The powdery material tumbled down into the ravine, and the huge packers did their work preparing a solid base for the footings and foundation of our church building. Gradually we saw the cement block walls go up and the roof go on, followed by the interior work, until at last our church family left the library to gather with praise and glory to God in the completed church building.

Kamloops proved to be a most interesting place in which to live.

When we had announced to our church family in Lively, Ontario, near Sudbury, that we were moving to Kamloops, some who had visited the area wondered why we would willingly choose to come to this hot, dry, dusty place.

For ourselves, we came to love looking across the East Trans-Canada highway, over the CPR train tracks and over the South Thompson river up into the hills. We loved those clay walls standing brown in the sun. The hoodoos carved by wind and erosion greeted our eyes on every trip up Barnhartvale Road or Todd Road while going to and coming from Barnhartvale.

We came to love the smell of the sagebrush, spreading its grey- green foliage over the dry landscape. I enjoyed pulling it through my fingers and inhaling its pungent aroma. We were told to watch out for rattlesnakes, but we never saw or heard one. We were also warned about ticks but although we saw ticks, we were never affected by one.

Kamloops Tapestry

Ducks and geese could be seen on the river almost all year, but we looked forward each fall to the sight of the beautiful white swans settling down on the water.

Although we couldn't see the salmon as they swam past us toward the Adams River, we did visit the spawning grounds. There the sea of red and green bodies spoke to us of the proliferation of the species through the death of the givers of eggs and sperm.

Building a home against a hill presented an interesting challenge. In order to get a back yard, a space for a garden, and a back driveway, the bulldozer cut away the hill to provide a fairly wide, level area accessible from the patio doors on the main floor.

Next, the excavator prepared three terraces, each six feet high, several feet wide and seventy-five feet long, cut into the clay, and rising up to the neighbours above us. This required the removal of 100 truckloads of soil, which were trucked to some site needing fill. Of course, those clay banks had to be stabilized against erosion, and so began a nine- year project of carrying stones home in the trunk of our car from wherever we could find them.

Using my day off and any spare moments, I broke those rocks with a sledgehammer. A cement mixer emptied load after load of mortar into a wheelbarrow to fasten those rocks into place, and ever so slowly, stone walls began to arise. After nine years, these walls all came to completion- just in time for us to sell the property and move to the lower mainland.

Yes, Kamloops became our home during those nine years. An indication of how we loved this city is seen in

Allen Hern

the fact that, after I had served as a pastor for twenty-two years my wife and I returned to this area once again. This time we purchased a home in Brocklehurst.

When we came to Kamloops in 1977, and even when we left in 1986, we did not believe we would ever want to live on the North Shore. It had appeared to be the poor sister of the rapidly expanding community. At that time Sahali and Aberdeen had become the new focal point.

But great changes have taken place in North Kamloops and Brocklehurst. So many new buildings, new businesses, and new homes are transforming the oldest section of Kamloops. Where once Brock was occupied by fields of orchards, now few fruit trees remain. They have been replaced by housing, a shopping centre, seniors' residences and care facilities.

Since returning, I have had the joy of serving as associate pastor at First Baptist, finally retiring in 2018 after 50 years in ministry.

Aaah, Kamloops! We crippled our way into your arms more than forty-two years ago, wondering if we were doing the right thing, but you have embraced us, held us and someday you will be our last resting place.

Out of all of British Columbia, we are glad that we yielded to your clay hills and lovely waterways.

Kamloops, we are happy to call you our home!

Allen Hern: retired after 50 years of ministry. Now enjoying the time to work on other projects - a book seeking a publisher about an extraordinary woman: **"Challenge and Change – the travails and joys of a complex woman".** Now working on a second book.

Alex McGilvery

TRANQUILLE DARK

By Alex McGilvery

Thursday April 25

    The fight started between two young punks as Blue walked toward the Duchess. The younger one, hardly more than a kid, quivered in rage as the other poked his chest. Whatever he was saying, the kid didn't like it He spun away and stomped in Blue's direction.

    The kid wasn't quite yelling—mostly swear words, as if they were the only thing to come to mind while he was angry. As he passed Blue, he sent a punch at Blue's face. The would be gang-banger's fist thudded against Blue's arms. The leather jacket absorbed most of the force. Undeterred, the kid kept swinging.

    His face showed his frustration as his friends called out a mix of encouragement and mockery. His dirty blond hair straggled past his shoulders partially hiding the unfinished tattoo. The guy this kid wanted to beat up leaned against the wall by the door of the Duchess, smoking and laughing. He tossed the cigarette on the ground and sauntered away.

    "Hey, kid." Blue lowered his arms slightly to catch the young man's eye. "Can we finish this up? I'd like to get a coffee to warm up."

    "Shut up, old man." The kid swung hard. Blue stepped to the side and let it pass over his shoulder. "No homeless freak is going to make a fool of me."

    Not like you need help with that.

Kamloops Tapestry

The kid's friends were getting bored. They wanted to see blood, maybe have a chance to land a few kicks of their own. If they swarmed him, it would be trouble. Blue already struggled to keep the beast on its leash.

The kid pulled a knife. It snicked open—a gas station karambit, cheap steel, crap quality, but it could still kill.

"Hank..." one of the hangers-on called out uncertainly, but another punched his arm with a warning glare then stared at Blue avidly.

Blue danced out of range and put a suitably nervous expression on his face. As he'd hoped when he saw the knife, Hank rushed in, slashing wildly. He had no idea how to use the blade.

Blue caught Hank's arm. To the people around, it would look like he was desperately holding off the kid's attack. Hank's wide eyes showed the pain in his arm had cut through the anger.

"Listen, Hank." Blue spoke softly so only Hank would hear him. "You've proved yourself to be tough. Say something nasty and threaten to really cut me next time, then walk away laughing."

"And if I don't?" Hank's eyes hardened. Blue increased the pressure on the arm.

"Then I break your arm and you look like an idiot who can't take an old man." He met Hank's eyes and let him catch a glimpse of the monster hiding behind them.

"Next time, I'll gut you for real," Hank shouted before stepping back. Blue released him, ready for another attack, but Hank spun away, replacing the knife in his back pocket. "I don't want the cops after me for some worthless bum."

Alex McGilvery

Blue sighed and waited until the group had walked away north toward Tim Horton's, forcing anyone in their path to jump aside. He'd get his coffee at Mac's today. Clenching and releasing his hands loosened the tension in his arms.

Damn, but I could use a drink. But then, when in the past two years had Blue not needed a drink? Caffeine would have to do.

Blue crossed the street and headed north. He pulled his beanie from a pocket in his coat and put it on. Not much of a disguise, but unless Hank was looking for him, it would get him past Timmies. His stomach grumbled. Maybe the Sally Ann would still have bread left. The change in his pocket wasn't enough for a muffin.

He almost stopped in at the Big Edition office, but this late in the month the paper didn't sell well.

Tranquille bustled like two streams that refused to mix. People in well-worn, dirty clothes and a crazy mix of layers passed those in clean clothes, which, if they had a tear, had been bought that way. Neither met the other's eyes, though they miraculously avoided collisions on the sidewalk.

A car honked at a man pushing a shopping cart overflowing with torn black bags and a cardboard sign reading "Bless you." The wave the man sent at the car didn't look like a blessing.

At the Sally Ann, a stale loaf of rye bread sat on the shelf. Blue picked it up, turned to see a woman eyeing it hungrily and nodded for her to follow him outside, where he took a handful of slices before passing the rest to her. On an impulse he gave her a free coffee coupon from the last two in his pocket.

She stuffed bread into her mouth. He nibbled at one of his slices.

"Thanks," she said with her mouth full.

Blue smiled and headed toward McDonald's. A coffee was calling his name. He ate the rye bread as he walked, tossing the last crust to a pair of crows.

The girl at the counter relaxed when he handed over the sticker-filled cardboard oval. The caffeine settled into his veins, helping him both relax and wake up properly. Blue sat in a far corner where management wouldn't spot him, though as long as he had the cup, he was likely safe enough.

"Hey." A man with a Santa Claus beard and tattooed arms slid in across from Blue. "You going to keep that sticker?"

Blue peeled it off and passed it over.

"What's up, Sam?"

"Different turkeys, same shit." Sam slurped at his coffee. It almost overflowed from the cream and sugar the man put into it. Blue drank his black and bitter.

"Ain't that the truth." Blue stretched and rolled his neck.

A youngster cried, high pitched and sharp, on the other side of the restaurant and Blue gripped his cup to keep his hands from shaking.

The youngster kept up its wailing, accompanied by a woman's cajoling voice.

"Gotta go." Blue stood and picked up his coffee. "Take care."

Outside he took a long pull at the coffee, wishing again for a drink. The chill breeze curled under his coat collar, making him shiver. Should have asked where Sam had seen Rooster; too late now.

To keep warm, Blue put his free hand in his pocket and headed toward the North Thompson.

The wind was sharper by the river, but after Blue clambered down toward the beach, he could walk along the path sheltered by the trees. The water covered the beach, but left a dry strip of brush. Though it was early in the season yet, he spotted more than one tent. One fight in a day was enough. He wouldn't risk being thought a trespasser, so he skirted around them.

He rounded the bend and walked under the Overlander Bridge then up the bank and over to MacDonald Park. Nothing gained but mud on his boots.

The upside was, he'd burned enough time to head to The Loop to see what they had on for lunch. He completed his circle back to Tranquille and pushed through the doors. It smelled good. Blue grabbed a plate and another coffee and tucked in. A few people gossiped over their meals, but most concentrated on eating the only food they'd get that day.

"What's up, Blue?"

"Not a lot, Jake." Blue leaned back to look up at the guy who ran the kitchen and kept things moving.

Jake slapped his back then moved on to talk to a couple of other regulars.

"You hear Ray OD'd?" A woman Blue didn't know was talking to a man on a scooter beside her.

"Ray?" The man shook his head. "Thought he was smarter than that."

"Not smart enough."

Someone pulled out a deck of cards and Blue played cribbage until closing, then helped Jake clean up for the day.

He should head back to his camp.

Almost at the Halston bridge, Blue reached up to tug on a rope, untying the knot. He lowered his bag to the ground, then tucked both ends of the rope out of sight. Back when he'd thought camping was just a fun activity, he'd learned to hide his gear in trees to keep it away from bears. It worked just as well for people; at least, no one had found it yet.

Across the river, the mountains glowed gold in the late afternoon light. Blue checked the pitiful supply of tinned food he had left. Good thing tomorrow was payday. He sat watching the geese until the sky darkened and the moon rose to reflect in the river.

The moon was a perfect circle, shining with silver light. It would be nice to live up there with no people around. Instead he was stuck down here with the reflection, troubled by the current. He shook the thoughts from his head and wrapped up in his bivouac bag, tent and sleeping bag in one.

He fell asleep with the sound of geese honking in the dark.

This is an excerpt from Tranquille Dark, edited for this collection.

Alex McGilvery

Alex has been reading since before he can remember and writing almost that long. He has published more than 20 books and is author and editor at his imprint Celticfrog Publishing. He lives in Kamloops with his dog and the stories clawing their way out of his head.

His most recent project is the new '*Blue in Kamloops*' series, with the first book *Tranquille Dark* being released this spring. More of his work can be found at alexmcgilvery.com

Kamloops Tapestry

KAMLOOPS
By Janet Miller

Tk'emlu'ps
Translation, Kamloops
Local Secwepemc Nation
1800's, European Explorers Arrived
Lakes, Canoes, Fishing and Hunting
Trading Pelts, Beads, Knives and Blankets
Rich in History, Culture and Natural Resources
Where the North and South Thompson Rivers Meet
Hoodoo Formations Surround Kamloops, Located Primarily in the Valley
Fur Traders, Gold Rush, Canadian Pacific Railway and Logging Industries
Hockey, Golfing, Curling, Parks, Galleries, Symphonies, Theatres and Museums
Art in the Park, Ribfest, Bands, Parades, Pow-Wows
Variety of Ethnic Cultures and Religious Groups
Thompson Rivers University, Mills and Agriculture
Pole Carvings and Wall Murals
Tournament Capital of Canada
Grasslands, Sagebrush, Tumbleweeds
Desert Temperatures
Home

This poem was the recipient of the first Dr. Robert and Elma Schemenauer Writing Awards in 2016 which is an annual writing contest through the Interior Authors Group in Kamloops, BC and their continued support is greatly appreciated. The poem "Kamloops" won in the category of Writing with a Kamloops Theme.

The poem was written in the "1-10, 10-1" form which I learned at a workshop held at the Downtown Kamloops Library from its creator, the late Richard Wagamese.

Janet Miller

Janet was born in Saskatchewan. She moved to the remote Islands of Haida Gwaii, in her early twenties. She lived there for nine years where she fell in love with British Columbia. She started writing poetry in her teens, and hasn't stopped. Besides travel and writing, some of her other passions include, stained glass, pottery, photography, and reading. She recently purchased a property on Vancouver Island, to spend time in solitude, and write. She is also a member of the Interior Authors Group. Janet and her family reside in Kamloops, British Columbia. Janet is currently working on a historical fiction novel.

KAMLOOPS? SERIOUSLY?

By Corea Ladner

I fell in love with Vancouver after moving there with my family in my childhood. As a teenager, our family returned to Toronto and I missed the west coast terribly. The magnificent mountain ranges and glaciers, vast conifer forests, huge waterfalls cascading over giant boulders; what an incredible world. I returned to Vancouver as a young adult to be in my true home. Eight years later, I discovered I had solar light deficiency, or Seasonal Affective Disorder (SAD). Through research, I discovered Vancouver receives approximately five and a half days of cloud cover average per week year-round. I spent four years trying different interventions to heal the SAD, but ultimately had to leave the coast for a sunnier place. This included time spent in Calgary and Winnipeg, where I got to appreciate how nice it is not to live through -45 C. winters.

I pined for the west, to be back in "my" mountains, "my" coastal rain forests, to be near the expansive magic of the Pacific Ocean seashore. However, my body couldn't handle the depression and the brain fog of a place with so little sunshine. I asked my Inner Guidance "Where should I go?" The answer "Kamloops". Kamloops? Seriously? Even its name is nerdy. Before moving here, whenever I thought of Kamloops, I thought of Fruitloops. I wondered why anyone would name a city as such and expect to be taken seriously. Afterwards I learned it was a real name derived from the local indigenous people's language meaning; "meeting of the waters, or meeting of the rivers." Mostly I remembered Kamloops as a very hot, very brown little town one had to get through on the way to the paradise of Vancouver.

Over the years I'd slowly begun to trust my Inner Guidance but moving to Kamloops was still unbelievable. I started with researching the city from a distance. Turns out that was a very good idea. It helped me to get past some of my prejudice about dusty, barren, landlocked little towns.

I discovered that Kamloops had grown into a cosmopolitan, sophisticated city. It had several positive attributes in every category of business, health facilities, job market, infrastructure, and other important areas.

It was time to pay a visit to the city in 2005. Touring around and seeing everything, I had to admit Kamloops was strangely beautiful. My favourite subjects were the mountains, forests and seashore of the west coast. Understandably, Kamloops with its relatively barren landscape was difficult to accept. That was a small disadvantage. Most importantly, it felt right to be here. I took the plunge and moved to Kamloops in 2006.

My spiritual sustenance comes essentially from my relationship to nature. Kamloops had mountains and almost limitless trails nearby. Check. Kamloops is the second sunniest city in BC. Check. The two rivers that form the hub of the city are clean with sandy bottoms. Oh boy. Years of swimming north of Toronto in Georgian Bay with wonderful sandy bottom beaches had spoiled me rotten. After leaving Georgian Bay, clean, sandy bottomed beaches were very rare. It was also necessary to travel some distance to get to them. Sandbars and sandy shorelines abound right in the heart of the Kamloops. I discovered I could leave work and WALK to the river for a refreshing dip after a hot workday. BIG check.

Being in Kamloops has been a gradual and gentle unfoldment of positive discovery. One of the key aspects was the existence of Thompson Rivers University (TRU). I had needed an educational upgrade for years. Finally, I obtained a Diploma there in Human Services (social work). This enabled me to finally find a job that was more fulfilling than anything I had done previously.

The diversity and quantity of sports facilities is amazing. I've always enjoyed sports and fitness activities. What came as a complete surprise is that Kamloops can claim to be "Canada's Tournament Capital." The city hosts 102 sports tournaments annually. That's an average of two tournaments per week. That's a lot for a little city. The pool and gymnasium at the Tournament Capital Centre are huge. Kamloops hosted the Canada Summer Games in 1993 with over 3,357 athletes and 8,400 volunteers. McArthur Island Sportsplex has three arenas under one roof, nine soccer fields and nine baseball pitches. I've never seen so many playing fields in one place. The entire island is devoted to sports. What a concept! It makes it very easy for the visiting athletes to get around, unlike the transportation challenges they face in the larger metropolitan areas.

Another aspect which continues to delight and amaze me is the Communities in Bloom program. I wasn't much of a flower appreciator until moving here. The colours, the variety of plants, the incredible designs blending flowers of such diversity are unprecedented. "People, plants and pride... growing together" is the Communities in Bloom slogan, and it captures the essence of the program - to foster civic pride, environmental responsibility and beautification through community involvement and the challenge of a national competition, with focus on the promotion and value of green spaces within urban settings. Kamloops has won a variety of accolades including Best Blooming Community – National Winners 2004, 2009, 2010 & 2012 and International Winners 2006 & 2013."

Hiking around the city has introduced me to the relatively foreign natural wonders of sagebrush, cacti, and tumbleweed. During the first few years I kept thinking I've only seen these in Hollywood westerns. Seeing their subtle hues and textures every season has helped me to appreciate their own unique beauty. By the very absence of forested areas, I have grown to appreciate even more the trees that are here. One tree that thrives is the prolific Ponderosa Pine. Many of these trees have trunks that are thicker than a refrigerator and stand eighty to a hundred feet tall. It is amazing how large they are, since the soil is rocky and receives little rain.

Kamloops has an approximate elevation gain of 1100 feet between the downtown and the residential area of Aberdeen on the southern ridge. There are many beautifully landscaped residential streets throughout the south ridge that slope down towards the river. A large part of this area has a beautiful name - Sahali. It is the local indigenous word for "high place". At night when one looks from the north across the river to this area, thousands of sparkling lights expand and rise up and up like long, languid waves. This magical view is so expansive and high, it seems like the city lives in the sky.

The clouds here are especially unique. When the conditions are just right, they look like soft flying saucers. Or even more peculiar, clouds here can have a completely straight edge. Some cloud god just took a knife and cut away a piece. All the clouds I've ever seen elsewhere have curved edges. Kamloops doesn't get a blanket of clouds as a routine weather pattern. Clouds here tend to be individualized, and they move fast. One cloud will suddenly appear over the Grasslands to the Northwest. It's dark gray, ominous, and heavy with moisture. Within minutes a curtain of rain slowly descends over Brocklehurst, but, it's sunny and clear over the rest of the city. The little rain squall is over, and the cloud is gone in half an hour. Then another one appears over Mt. Paul. It's slightly mauve, larger and shaped completely differently. Within minutes it looms over the downtown, threatening to rain but ultimately does not. It too is gone in half an hour. This parade of remarkably different clouds and their activity can go on all day. Sometimes three separate clouds can be raining in three different spots! There's so much visual variety over Kamloops, that I refer to it as "sky theatre."

Kamloops is so different from the other cities in which I've lived. If you had told me before discovering Kamloops that someday I'd move to this little city I would have laughed at you. Not anymore. Kamloops has the nicest climate in which I've lived. I can hike in the mountains just by taking a bus up the hill to Kenna Cartwright Park. It's the largest municipal park in BC, occupying eight square kilometres of Mt. Dufferin, with over forty km of trails through open grasslands and forest.

The people here are the friendliest I've ever met. It's possible to meet a friend whenever stepping out the door to simply go grocery shopping. For a big city gal, it's amazing to keep bumping into people, having a smile and a greeting, feeling a real sense of community. The job commute is fifteen minutes, the air is clear, the river is clean. The neighbourhood is safe, the mountains look magnificent in snow and in spring.

Kamloops? Seriously? Yes! Yes, indeed.

Corea Ladner is a social worker with special needs clients. In high school and university she wrote a lot of A+ essays, according to the teachers. She went on to edit grant proposals at the University of Manitoba. As a Toastmaster for 5 years, she wrote and delivered many speeches, one of which she delivered in the annual Toastmaster's International Speech Contest. Corea won the competition at four levels, allowing her to represent BC at the Toastmaster's Regional Championship. Corea loves dogs and cats, playing the piano and laughing. Her balcony has five trees.

Elma Schemenauer

RETURNING TO KAMLOOPS

By Elma (Martens) Schemenauer
   Returning to Kamloops to teach at the arts camp brought memories of Florian Bouchard rushing back. Our time together had kindled a fire that still smouldered in my heart ten months later.
   I'd never visited the university campus with Florian, but as I taught embroidery and crocheting under the cottonwood trees, I wondered if Florian had sat under those same trees, and with whom. When I ate in the cafeteria, I wondered which tables Florian had sat at and what he had eaten. At the same time, I scolded myself for playing dangerous mind games, or heart games. I was a married woman.
   The pottery shop where Florian worked was only twelve blocks from the university. I could take a bus there or walk. Obviously, I shouldn't.
   Maybe Florian would find me. He had to know I was in Kamloops. The arts camp had been widely advertised. My name was on posters and in *Kamloops This Week*, along with those of the other instructors.
   I waited ten days for Florian to contact me. Nothing. Maybe he was out of town or married. Probably not married. My friend Bella would have heard about it and told me.
   On the third Friday of the camp, the campers and instructors were going hiking at Sun Peaks. They planned to sketch wildflowers and wildlife. The

mountain venue didn't seem suitable for teaching needlework so I begged off.

After the hikers left, I took the bus downtown. Florian's shop didn't open till ten, so I wandered the streets for a while. It felt good to stroll those familiar streets. Not much had changed since I'd left. Most of the shops were the same, selling clothing, jewellery, kitchen wares and hand-crafted items. Complementing this mix were restaurants and coffee shops, the library and several art galleries.

At ten o'clock, I headed up First Avenue toward the pottery shop. It was a red-brick building with a green door. The window displayed bowls, mugs and teapots. I peered inside but didn't see anyone. I turned and walked around the block, mustering my courage and puffing a bit because the streets were steep.

At ten-fifteen I stopped in front of the green door, calmed my breathing and eased the door open. As I stepped inside, a buzzer sounded and Florian hurried in through a back door. He jumped as if he'd been shot. "What are you doing here?"

I gave him a sideways look, little-girl style. "I was just passing by. I thought I'd stop and say hello." He probably knew this was a lie.

Florian fingered the ceramic cross he wore over his smock. "Is your husband here? What about Emily and Noreen?" He looked thinner than before, his jaw more pronounced.

"The girls are with their grandma in Saskatchewan, and Simon's in Nova Scotia, touring with a band."

"So you're alone in Kamloops."

I smiled. "I've been alone here almost three weeks, unless you count everyone else at the camp. I expected to have run into you by this time."

Florian tightened the leather thong that held his ponytail in place. "I tried hard to ensure that wouldn't happen." His voice sounded stiff and formal.

"Why? Didn't you want to see me? Too busy?" If he still cared for me, he would have found time.

He gave me a bleak smile. "That's not it."

"Are you engaged?"

"No, not engaged, not married." He glanced toward the back door. "You'll have to excuse me. I need to unload the kiln."

"So what should I do? Leave?" He was blowing me off like dandelion fuzz. How could he do that, after what we'd meant to each other?

Florian gave me an unreadable look. "Yes, I think leaving would be your best option." He turned and disappeared through the back door.

I hesitated a moment, then followed. He owed me an explanation, if nothing else.

The door was heavy. I struggled through it and found myself in a large, screened-in veranda. A ceramic kiln dominated the room. Several racks stood nearby. A laundry sink crouched in one corner.

Without even a glance in my direction, Florian put on gloves, cracked the door of the kiln open, waited a few moments and then opened the door wider. A wave of heat rolled toward me. I stepped into it, longing to share it with Florian.

He nudged me away. "Careful. You don't want to get burned."

"I won't." Narrowing my eyes against the heat, I peered into the kiln at rows of pottery on shelves. Bowls, teapots, candle-holders, crucifixes, vases shaped like mermaids with wavy hair tumbling over their tails.

"Did you make any of those?" I asked.

"Nope." Florian reached into the kiln and removed a teapot made in the shape of a clock. "I don't do pottery." He pulled one of the racks closer and set the teapot on it.

"So who made them?"

"My boss and his daughters."

I wondered if the daughters were pretty. Charming?

Florian's jaw tightened. "Could you get out of my way, please?"

I retreated to the corner by the sink. "Are you still making sculptures?" I asked, leaning against the sink. "I read about your 'hypnotic eye' series."

Florian removed a blue pitcher from the kiln. Did his hand tremble, or was that my imagination? "No, I've moved out of my 'hypnotic eye' phase."

"Yeah?"

"I'm doing a modern-day depiction of Blessed Sibyllina Biscossi."

"Who?"

"A blind Italian saint who lived in the 1300s."

"That's a switch," I said.

"It is."

"You're kidding, right?"

"Nope, not kidding." Florian removed a mermaid vase from the kiln, flicked a bit of extra glaze off her tail and set her on the rack. "I've changed since you saw me last."

"It would seem so." Ten months ago, Florian had been my charming bad boy, tempting me to break my marriage vows. Now he was… What?

Florian straightened the cross that hung around his neck. "I've returned to our Lord Jesus Christ."

I blinked. "Pardon me?"

"I've returned to our Lord, and to the Holy Catholic Church and the sacraments."

"Really?" Ten months ago I had refused Florian's advances because of my faith. Now he was the religious one.

"It would be a sin for me to come between you and your husband—"

The buzzer sounded. "Excuse me." Florian hurried out into the shop. "May I help you?"

"Is Albert around?" A man's voice, Eastern European.

Florian closed the door on me.

I slumped against the sink. Florian's faith was different from mine, but he made me realize how far I'd strayed from my Mennonite principles. I should probably disappear from his life, just slip away into the back alley.

But it would be rude to run off without saying goodbye, wouldn't it? As I was trying to decide, Florian burst back into the veranda. "Just what I need, more work." His voice rasped with irritation. "Tibor's Restaurant needs forty candle-holders by three-thirty. I've got to find 'em, pack 'em, pack all this other stuff, deliver the candle-holders and then drive all the way to Salmon Arm."

"What's in Salmon Arm?"

"Artisan market tomorrow."

"Could I help you pack?"

"Nope." Florian removed a brown teapot from the kiln and set it on the rack with the other pottery.

I grabbed my purse. "I guess I should run along."

"Yes, you should." Florian removed several mugs from the kiln, almost dropping one.

"Okay." I tried to sound like my heart wasn't splitting in two. "I'll be on my way then."

Florian turned his back on me. Were his shoulders shaking?

"Are you all right?" I asked.

"I'm fine." His voice sounded strangled.

"Are you sure?"

"I don't want you to go."

His voice was so quiet, I wasn't sure I'd heard right. "Pardon me?"

"I said I don't want you to go."

I felt like a condemned prisoner pardoned at the last second. "Why not?"

"Because I'm crazy about you."

As fireworks exploded in my heart, a brown station wagon rumbled into the alley.

Florian clattered the mugs onto a rack. "That'll be Albert." His words rushed out. "I'm booked into a hotel in Salmon Arm, the smaller one by the lake. Meet me there, would you? Six thirty."

"What for?"

"Dinner, just dinner."

I swallowed shooting stars. "No, I'd better not. You just said it would be wrong to—"

"Please? We've gotta talk."

"I'll think about it." I bolted away, struggled with the door and fled out through the shop into the street.

Florian Bouchard still loved me! Every nerve in my body tingled with excitement. Adrenaline pushing me along, I set off on foot, heading for the university—I didn't have the patience to wait for the bus.

It wouldn't be so terrible to meet Florian for "just dinner," would it? I wouldn't go up to his room with him, wouldn't climb those red-carpeted stairs even if he begged me to. I was strong enough to resist, wasn't I?

Kamloops Tapestry

By Elma (Martens) Schemenauer

GOLD AND ROSES

In 1862 rich deposits of gold were found in the Cariboo Mountains 400 km (250 mi) north of Kamloops.

Prospectors flocked to the area, especially from California, where a gold rush had recently ended.

Elma Schemenauer

MEANWHILE Overlanders from the east headed for the Cariboo. Catherine & Augustus Schubert travelled with their 3 young children.

Catherine was the only woman. Augustus had wanted her to stay in the Red River Colony (now Winnipeg), especially since she was pregnant.

She insisted on going.

The Overlanders travelled by Red River cart.

Kamloops Tapestry

Wild roses were an important part of their diet along the way.

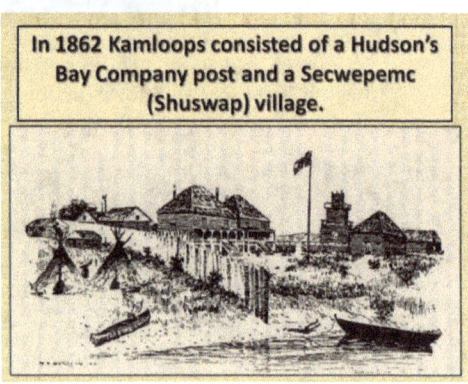

In 1862 Kamloops consisted of a Hudson's Bay Company post and a Secwepemc (Shuswap) village.

The Schuberts reached Kamloops October 12, 1862. Catherine was the first non-Indigenous woman to enter BC from the east.

Elma Schemenauer

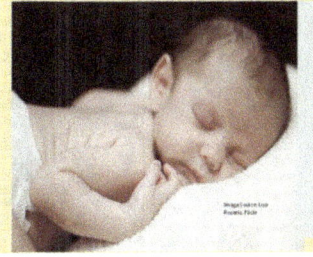

On October 13, 1862, the Schuberts' daughter Rose was born in the village.

Rose may have been the first non-Indigenous child born in the BC Interior.

Schubert Drive in Kamloops is named for the Schubert family.

The Overlander Bridge & Park are named for the Overlanders including the Schuberts.

Elma (Martens) Schemenauer is the author of many books including *YesterCanada: Historical Tales of Mystery and Adventure* and the 1940s-era Mennonite novel *Consider the Sunflowers*, both published by Borealis Press of Ottawa. She grew up in Saskatchewan; taught in Saskatchewan, Montana, and Nova Scotia; and worked as an editor and writer in Toronto for many years. Elma now lives on a sagebrush-dotted mountainside in Kamloops. For more, please visit http://elmams.wix.com/elma

Kamloops Museum and Archives

PHOTOS FROM THE ARCHIVES

Lorne Street showing north side – part of block 100, 200, and first part of 300 block – with original Royal Inland Hospital near the right end. Photo of early 1890s.

KMA 1381

Wooden bridge of C.N.R. over North Thompson in course of erection 1913; replaced by another structure.

Kamloops Tapestry

A 475 (G.C. Scatchard collection)

Royal Inland Hospital, 1921.   *KMA 189*

Tranquille in the mid-1920s.

KMA 1707 (R.G. Pinchbeck collection)

Kamloops Museum and Archives

C.N.R. Kamloops Junction station, ca. 1930s.

KMA 8944 (accession # 1772.050.030)

At the C.P.R. crossing.

KMA 3585 (G.D. Brown collection)

View across the bridge to North Kamloops.

KMA 3586 (G.D. Brown collection)

Mail sorting room, Old Federal Building (Victoria Street West), May 29, 19__? *KMA 5515*

Kamloops Museum and Archives

C.R. Lamb on the Thompson River at Kamloops, in 1932.
KMA 1705 (R.G. Pinchbeck collection)

Wing Building, corner of Victoria Street and 3rd Avenue, Kamloops, completed and opened June 1948. *KMA 1779*.

Kamloops Tapestry

B.C. Coach Lines Depot at 235 Lansdowne Street.
KMA 1783.

Ellsay Bros. grocery store and post office, 29 Tranquille Road.
KMA 1846.

Kamloops Museum and Archives

Dominion Hotel, Victoria Street West, Kamloops, December 1949. *KMA 1854.*

New Paramount Theatre at corner of 5th Avenue and Victoria Street during construction, September 1954. *KMA 4081*

Kamloops Tapestry
WHAT THE CROWS SAY

By Eleanor Hancock

The crows are in collusion with the Government, I'll bet, over the fate of the garden--that's Peterson Creek Community Garden on Columbia St. Well they'll be sorry when we're gone.

No more dive-bombing as we bend over in spring; no more tender shoots to nibble off. Yes, we know you're the superior bird, the Air Canada magazine on the plane said so, I read it, pages and pages--too long.

You're cackling in the tall fir right now, probably sneering as we sweat below in the garden. Receiving text messages from Victoria? etc.

Chief Gardener Jim, glares at them, shakes his fist. They're cockier these days, makes us suspicious.

The word is the Government is taking back their land next year, and in midseason if they feel like it. Well thank you very much, taking back their land? Whose land? What's going to happen to the land? Development? Nobody tells us anything. I've been a gardener here for years; we'll probably have to read about it in *Kamloops This Week*. The government is supposed to inform Shannon Gourlay, manager of city community gardens. Just whose land is it, anyway?

Crows - normally I like crows, but it's June 2 and 36 degrees Celsius and the Government has only now turned on the water to our individual plots. Eleven plots waiting for water, day after day. I've been putting off planting, expecting to have to give away the bedding plants, veggies languishing at home on the balcony for

Eleanor Hancock

nearly three weeks: tomatoes, eggplant, phallic zucchinis-to-be... longing to get their feet into real dirt.

My business trip is exactly one week away, the water's on and I'm frantically laying out hoses and setting the automatic watering. Beets and carrots and beans still have to be seeded. (Tough beans! squawk the crows.) Organic rabbit manure from a rabbitty home in Westsyde is dug in, thankfully.

Other community gardens, from Sahali, to the Old Yacht Club, to the Airport, have had water for weeks. They're on city water, but Peterson Creek Community Garden is on Government Water; and Government Water gets turned on from Vernon. Yes! Vernon!

The excuse was a break in the line at the neighbours, the Law Courts' lawn. We don't believe it, no lawn torn up for repairs. We don't believe the Government.

People started hauling water from home, and a pioneering couple actually appeared with a shiny metal pail and rope to draw water from Peterson Creek. In desperation, Jim and Shannon Gourlay ran a hose through the fence from an outlet at the sidewalk on Columbia Street. Water!

We're on Government Land on Columbia Street, between Fifth and Sixth Avenue, flanked by old government buildings, equipment compounds and parking lots on both sides of Peterson Creek which runs right alongside the garden. Some buildings look almost vacant, semi-cared-for, which makes us suspicious too. Development?

Being interested in Kamloops' history, I looked about. The building behind the garden is vacant; it was

Kamloops Tapestry

Highways until a year ago; computers and Highwaymen faced us in the garden. Behind Highways is Ministry of Transportation and Infrastructure where the office manager knows little about the buildings — and the fate of things — but advised that the pristine building way back behind the Law Courts houses everything from soup to nuts, and might know.

Sure enough, there was Front Counter BC, Ministry of Forests, Lands and Natural Resource Operations and much, much more. I got the name of a retired forester who knows a lot. I called twice but no answer.

The City Archives tried to help, had nothing really, and recommended Victoria.

I went to Diane. Diane is a librarian at the downtown library a few blocks away, Victoria St. at Fifth Ave. Diane grew up in the yellow three-storey house at the corner of Nicola St. and Fifth, within spitting distance of the garden. Before she started school at the end of the 1950s, she and her little cronies ran wild, exploring; they knew all the nooks and crannies.

(Her family home stands beside my apartment building on Nicola; her father died and the house is for sale. Diane and hubby live just over on Sixth, alongside Peterson Creek. The Creek flows under Columbia and Nicola, and emerges alongside their property, albeit in a concrete bed, making its way to the Thompson River.)

Diane didn't know the garden is going to go, or what would become of the land. She suggested Kamloops-South Thompson Liberal MLA Todd Stone's office across the street from the library. (Todd was Minister of Highways until the last election.)

Eleanor Hancock

The present working forestry building, with heritage designation, says Diane, was never ever the Provincial Home for Old Men, it was always Forestry. Going west, the Old Men's Home was two over, on the site of today's Ponderosa Lodge care facility between Law Courts and Royal Inland Hospital.

Since I served as editor of the Kamloops Museum Association's newsletter for 11 years, and on the Board twice, I recalled the Old Men's Home opened soon after Kamloops' 1893 incorporation on John Ussher's former farm, and housed old-timers: gold miners, guides, fur trappers; many are buried just up Sixth Avenue in the Old Men's Cemetery; some were in the Barkerville gold rush. (In 1879, Johnny Ussher, who was Government Agent and Constable, was killed by the Wild McLeans.)

Expanses of lawn, shade trees and lovely flower beds showcase the Columbia Street buildings-- Forestry, Law Courts, Ponderosa Lodge.

The Law Courts was the site of the old RCMP station, says Diane, with jail in basement, office on main floor, and warden and his wife and grandchildren living upstairs. Little Diane and her buddies would collect up the kids and race off on their exploring agenda, while jail inmates might be gardening in the jail's garden behind

Going east, the huge building on Columbia across from Denny's Restaurant, was never ever a stables, says Diane, it was Highways. The hard-to-decipher sign, I said, reads BC MailPlus, and it seemed deserted, a warehouse, maybe, until I peeked in the window and saw a person at work.

Too bad! I loved the idea of an old stables!

The attractive stone wall with a little centrepiece fountain and out-of-control shrubbery was torn down four years ago to move the sidewalk back.

(The vacant Highways right behind the garden, says Diane, used to be Motor Vehicles.)

So what, exactly, does the Government intend? Townhouses? Raze the buildings, tear out the garden, chop down the impressive cedar hedge towering alongside, along the Creek where street people sleep concealed and cool? Prime location, yes, Columbia St. Plus a creek.

We'll miss the garden—work, yes, planting darling teeny-tiny carrot seeds that stick to the fingers in blazing sun and are watered immediately by the sweat dripping from the end of the nose.

Sure, there's friction as in any family. (My hose dripped a lot at the tap at first and created flooding. And my open compost pit attracted the crows to Lily's tender shoots, she said, in no uncertain terms.) There's vandalism and theft and garden shed break-ins, despite locks and a higher fence.

The crows couldn't care less, easy pickings elsewhere, they chortle; tasty seedlings to be got at gardens nearby.

Don't they realize the very foundations of Canada are shaking: agriculture, place, identity? Enshrined in The Constitution, Charter of Rights and Freedoms. The crows are not for the little guy.

A NEWS FLASH ?

September 10. Diane emailed MLA Todd Stone's office, who contacted the City. City Parks Department

Eleanor Hancock assures there is no Peterson Creek Community Garden closure.

Well, their heart is in the right place but City Parks is not privy to Government information like this; ours is a community garden on Government land, not City land. Shannon Gourlay will contact us in September when she hears. Thanks anyway, Diane.

End

Notes

The article's title pays homage to acclaimed Canadian writer Robert Kroetsch, author of What the Crow Said.

Kamloops Tapestry

Eleanor grew up in a general store business at Zeballos, a landlocked logging town on Vancouver Island. From 1938 to 1943, Zeballos hosted Canada's last significant gold boom. Her grandfather, Seth Witton, purchased the store in 1939.

Captain James Cook, too, landed practically on their doorstep in 1778, but her interest centers on the 1930s.

Eleanor is the author of *Salt Chuck Stories from Vancouver Island's West Coast— Zeballos, Nootka Sound, Kyuquot*, now in its fourth printing. Last year she completed a book about the early stages of the boom, *Hardly the Klondike—the 1938 Zeballos Gold Boom*, that is being considered for publication.

Rita Joan Dozlaw
A PORTRAIT OF PRECOCIOUS

By Rita Joan Dozlaw

I fell in love at someone's wedding outside the
South Thompson Inn on Shuswap Road. It was
the late '90s, and I stood around in sand avoiding
all the staring eyes—especially hers, the girl
in the organza gown. My eyes eventually snared hers
when wind flared her shear hem, making her frown.
A satin belt, clutching her winsome waist, matched
her dark hair. She was stunning standing there as her
head fell back when, out loud, she finally laughed.

You would fall in love, as I, with her amber eyes
shining like the crystal beads at her nervous
neck. Just like the song, "The first time ever…" Her
face was imprinted on my soul. Framed in a coral
sun-bonnet, with those ringlets sneaking shyly
onto her precocious face, she was breathtaking. A
coronet of faux flowers, on a green velvet band,
matched the colours of the fragrant real ones
 she clutched in her genteel hand.

I could see her fingertips had been dipped in pink
ink—not just paint, but polished like her soul,
sort of transparent. I thought, at the time, *I'll never
again see such a beauty as her!* She tapped her toes
to surf-songs echoing over the river and fidgeted:
couldn't be still; asked repeatedly, how much
longer, and she gazed at them; not me, oh

Kamloops Tapestry

woe, how I fell for her heart-warmed lips, rosy as
sun rising over the poufy ruffles at her hips.

In a sacred moment, with eyes closed, I knew
I could forever devour her whole being. I wished
to wrestle her down on the playground; so
uncomfortable was I at the beachside affair with
love in the air. I suffered: in a bow-tie; carrying
wedding rings; and pre-adolescent feelings... Back
 then, she, the flower girl with a swirl of a smile, walked
with me down the aisle before I walked among men...
When I was only eleven and she was only ten.

Rita Joan Dozlaw

PEACE O' MIND

By Rita Joan Dozlaw

Boy, now that I am eighty, I cackle cuz I'm not shy
At Kamloops' grocers, baby. In purple, I catch one's eye!
He lugs my sack o' goodies, pushes shopping cart to car,
Gives quarters back to foodies—so we need not walk so far!
Old is gold cuz I don't cook in ovens or barbecues.
As a guest, I read a book, while families pay their dues.
I wear thick stockings, ear muffs, and fuzzy caps of warm wool.
Stamina, I've got enough—although I don't look too cool.

I get real bushed as night falls. "Are you sure you're okay, Mom?"
My doting sons make house calls. "Yeah, I've just ousted 'Old Tom.'
He's prob'ly stalkin' a mouse! *I* drank all his rich warm milk.
I heat only half the house. How dumb it is to wear silk.
It wrinkles awful in bed! So, now it ain't no matter,
I wear flannelette instead even though it don't flatter.
I'm interesting, I'm told, but slower gettin' around.
I'm waited on, never scolded, handy-dash takes me to town.

It's fun to have those grandkids catering. I'm patronized.
At dinner I get first dibs—yeah, I know I'm idolized.
You bet because I'm so old, I get away with too much.
I love winters e'en though cold, cuz dear ones stay close in touch.
It isn't often at all that anyone turns me down,
And when I'm sick or I fall, my kinfolk rally around.

Kamloops Tapestry

They stroke my old wiener dog; they never do seem to mind
That I am in such a fog! My family's really kind!

I'm grateful to get this old. It's easier now than then;
For, I'm getting really bold in seniors' homes where I've been.
Young folks come and collect me after I play pickle ball.
They seldom e'er neglect me, relieved that I rarely fall!
Shove extras in my back pack; for bridge games, I use my head.
My prerogative, in fact, lets me change my mind instead
Of playing by all the rules—also, pump high on my swing.
My heart's a garden of tools; for really, I'm in my 'spring'!"

I know I'm not a nuisance cuz kids never have said so.
They help me out, for instance. All I need's to let 'em know.

So, when I want a helper, they send willing grandkids out
To clean my humble shelter. Old is gold without a doubt!

LADY THOMPSON

By Rita Joan Dozlaw

Our lady, the South Thompson River, rolls unpretentiously past
Scalloped hems of shore—her shallows darkening dramatically
Beneath overhanging silver-grey Russian olives in the lustre
Of summer. Writhing by, she stretches her flawless legs and torso
Like a lithe yoga instructor. Taking no effort to push against
Strong winds, her own strengths are, of course, oblivious; for, they
Are well hidden in her underwater currents—as any woman's.

Our beautiful local river fills one's mind with intrigue; one's senses
With supernatural perception. What is beneath her whirlpools?
Where is she going in such a hurry? Where are her wings attached?
She appears to fly over unseen currents—that chameleon
Reflecting feathered faces of herons, bald eagles and gulls as they
Dodge sky-high jet-vapor trails, choppers and free-flying gliders
And carve their peculiar personalities on the firmament.

One very obvious charm: born to sing; never to be silenced;
Our Lady Thompson warbles rhythmically from her
Glazed stage like a soprano with glossy laughing eyes, and she
Cries with temperamental rain-clouds rushing to conjoin at the

Kamloops Tapestry

Horizon. Spiraling gulls call the river's name. They dive for morsels
Afloat on her white-knuckled fingers and white-capped shoulders.
This gracious hostess welcomes all nature and water lovers.

Ducks on parade linger with their young upon her wide lap.
Their webbed feet tease and tickle her underbelly, causing her
To wantonly rear her crowning glory and allow her rippled hair
The freedom to flow behind as she dodges rocks and reefs. What
An exotic dancer she is! En pointe, staging a boiling rage, she
Commands, in mesmerizing ballerina encores, a punctuation,
And penetrates deep dimples into whirlpool cheeks.

Entrapment and power, in one body, captures the human spirit,
And steadily, supremely flows away away, away with it. A
Swooshing voice echoes between foothills. O, such compulsion of
Worshippers following her songs, blind to the tempest, to embrace
Her natural world; spiral in a dream state pillowed by the buoyant
Depths of her pulsing universe of seduction, to vanish, in one's
Mind, into the watery secrecy of Lady Thompson's rolfing bosom.

Rita Joan Dozlaw
INTRODUCING: SUZETTE ROCHE AT THE SAGEBRUSH THEATRE

By Rita Joan Dozlaw

Suzette Roche entered the Sagebrush Theatre in Kamloops, followed by her music teacher Mrs. Major. Down the aisles, on the stage, stood the most beautiful concert piano Suzette had ever seen in her years of classical training. The Conreid New York Baby Grand dignified centre stage like no other in Suzette's memory. Its stunning colour, high-gloss-white, contrasted with the floor's highly-polished black hardwood. From her vantage point on stage, the twenty-two year old scanned the waves of the red sea, as she called them—the auditorium's rows of cranberry-red upholstered seats—parted by passages leading to Suzette's "dry-runs." Soon the deep sea would be filled with a bubbling mass of music lovers.

With time to relax before her evening concert, Suzette hailed a cab. She enjoyed getting around a bit while in Kamloops. Thanks to her win at a Montreal music competition, she was awarded funds which helped defray her travel expenses.

"Where to, ma'am?" The cabbie asked when he put his Sudoku puzzle aside.

"I've heard the down town Riverside Park is a beauty spot."

"Absolutely, ma'am. I can get you there in five minutes."

Kamloops Tapestry

It was June 2017, and Suzette strolled among the blooms and along the beach of the South Thompson River. She wandered under leafy canopies of beechnut trees and marveled at the large oak and mature maple heritage trees highly valued in the beautiful park. Finally, she sat in the rose garden, sniffed peach-coloured favourites and pulled her journal out. *"This is what I imagine –a huge wave, like a surge of surf, boiling over the 'red sea'—when all the patrons stand up."*

That evening, Suzette and her dear "Madge" arrived by cab at the Sagebrush. A sign of the hour of gloaming appeared in the glistening of the street lamp-lights which blinked on. Their soft glow seeped through the float-glass windows and into the lobby of the theatre.

"If I had fears, they've disappeared in the ambience here," Suzette said to Madge. "It will be an exhilarating experience to perform on that piano." Earlier in the day, when she practiced, its ethereal tones echoed in the fine acoustics of the vaulted ceiling. Hyped with excitement, she asked her devoted side-kick, "Did you notice the tall tapers on the parson-style table just inside the stage entrance? They'll flicker, and their dance will create fascinating images on the wall."

"Yes, I noticed. You're such a romantic, Suzette."

They entered the stage wing, and Suzette touched the soft nap of a stage drape side-panel. Her sensual heart leapt; for, she recalled the smooth texture of the rose petals she'd caressed earlier. She peeked behind one of the black velvet panels and gazed at the magnificent grand piano awaiting the gentle seduction of her ruby fingertips. She looked down at them, tightly closing in a fist and opening wide, confident her strong fingers would overpower the irresistible eighty-eight keys and, in total control, master their voices.

Rita Joan Dozlaw

The moment arrived to step onto the stage. Dignified and professional Suzette imagined herself princess-like, in a filigree and rhinestone tiara, making an impressive entrance. The anticipated wave of the sea, which she'd scribed in her journal, came to pass. A contagious welcome from over six-hundred patrons took her aback by standing and applauding. In response, acknowledging her adoring audience, she bowed and strands of auburn hair fell over her tear-filled eyes. "Thank you, everyone," she said with heartfelt sincerely.

Passing the parson's table, she picked up the personal ornate hourglass she left near the candles earlier that day. Turning it over, she set it right back down then, looking down at her crisp taffeta gown, she pinch-lifted a corner of it to avoid letting it brush the floor. She sat with poise, stoic and still, on the sleek white artist bench and watched the sand release rhythmic movements of time, grain by grain. She took the final moment to reveal her patent-leather slippers. They would get their jollies playing tootsie with the piano's three toes of brass.

Nothing was rushed. Everything was hushed. The main drapery of shimmering burgundy velour cascaded like waterfalls from the proscenium arch. The aura of her rose corsage, with its magical vernacular of fragrance, whispered, *my scent is wafting over this grand music chamber!* She felt her heart grinning and hoped it wasn't causing her cheeks to flush and expose her shyness.

When the sand in the timepiece mounded, she leaned her alabaster forehead over the rich ebony and ivory shelf and endowed it with her personal invocation of joy. Her eyes were downcast as in a sacred ritual... of laying of hands. The silent orchestration of her gestures exposed a reverent nature while the blest keys subtly reflected prisms of the crystal chandelier. It had been installed specifically for Suzette's performance.

Kamloops Tapestry

What surprises had she brought to the occasion? Only the adjacent support buttress was privy to her somber heart's prelude—*Let this music create an extraordinary eve to remember.* With one last glance over the crowd, her hazel eyes were mesmerized by the splay of colours and shapes connecting the whole auditorium like a massive jigsaw puzzle. She felt her hands burn with excitement as they took over the keyboard. Revelling in inconceivable energy, they worked their contortions in the opening piece, and the house rocked.

From the wings, Suzette's keen teacher heard the rhythmic 3/4 beat and a chill moved down her spine; for, she recognized her student's phenomenal rendition of... "What?" She could hardly contain her angst. *Chopsticks?* She thought, *that's not the introductory piece announced in the official program pamphlets!*" Then, she heard her name.

"Mrs. Major, would you join me on stage, please... " Suzette called after ending her super-fun selection to a deafening applause of approval. She introduced her teacher then asked her, "How did you like my piece?"

The guest to the stage curtsied and confirmed, "That was sensational...," but stalled. Her lips quivered slightly, yet she was compelled to further address the musician's choice of music.

"Your unplanned selection was extremely entertaining, Miss Roche... however, didn't we decide that the classical work you practiced to perfection would be your opening piece?"

In front of the full house, Suzette explained, "Yes, of course, but I chose 'Chopsticks' to warm up on. I learned to improvise with that one when I was a little girl. It's my favorite little waltz and the most played piano song, you know. Didn't you coach me to have fun?" The audience roared at the carefree dialogue and, with curiosity, watched Suzette open the piano bench. "May I please take one more liberty, Mrs. Major? ...with your consent and help?"

"Of course, dear. This is your concert."

"It is also our house-guest's concert!"

Mrs. Major's eyes shifted to the surprised audience. Their chuckles turned to audible laughter when Suzette gestured for help to undo a tightly-folded bundle. Together, shaking out the exquisite red and white nylon material, the women unraveled a custom-made gold-fringed party banner with the number 150 embroidered under a red maple leaf. A growing crescendo of hoots and whistles, from patrons of the arts, rose like crashing waves over that sea of puzzle pieces when Suzette and Mrs. Major draped the four-and one-half feet by seven feet banner over the open lid of the piano.

She announced, with a play on her friend's name, "Now, for an interactive major selection, we'll begin with *O Canada*. Would everyone please stand for our national anthem?"

On that warm June eve of Canada's 150th Anniversary of Confederation, hundreds of Kamloopsians sang their hearts out in the Sagebrush Theatre. If the bright stately banner muffled the piano in the least, it was not evident; for, the instrument's bravado magnificently enriched and heightened the sense of celebration and patriotism in the citizens' voices.

During the unforeseen prolonged ovation, the ladies removed the celebratory banner from the piano and a stage-hand retrieved it. Finally the musician's skilled hands rose from her lap to masterfully manhandle the slick keys. Typically talking to herself in secret, she declared, *these moments feel profoundly wonderful*... and the real drama began. Her fingers teased and tickled the ivories without flaw, and she pulled off a phenomenal concert on the spectacular concert piano... not by the book but by her extraordinary memory of contemporary classics officially listed on the program.

Kamloops Tapestry

Suzette's encore selection was a French tune she favoured at ten: *Au Clair de la Lune*. She extended the version to Claude Debussy's, *Clair de Lune*, a piece favored by classical pianists. In the lyrics of the children's chorus, *Pierrot*, in the light of the moon, looks for a pen then closes a door. Later backstage before leaving, Madge, extremely proud of her student, told her so then closed the door. Suzette found her pen and scribed the satisfaction they felt as the enthralled concert-goers dispersed under a full summer moon in Kamloops, B.C.

Rita Joan Dozlaw

Since her youth, Rita Joan Dozlaw has been a hobby writer. Following a thirty-five year secretarial career, her writings appeared in anthologies by: New Authors Journal; Famous Poets Society; Poetry Institute of Canada; and, The Poetry Guild. She's a regular monthly contributor of stories and poems in two local newspapers, has her own bi-line in a weekly out-of-town newspaper and writes frequently for a monthly out-of-province senior paper. As an active member of the Interior Authors Group in Kamloops, Dozlaw was twice honoured by the Dr. Robert and Elma Schemenauer Award, 2017/2019, for writing showing appreciation of nature.

Kamloops Tapestry

DYLAN'S DAY

By Ward Pycock

"Ladies and Gentlemen—Dylan Armstrong!" CBC broadcaster Scott Russell, the master of ceremonies, declared.

"Dylan! Dylan!" erupted the voices of a thousand fans decked out in their prominent red-and-white Canadian sports apparel. Dylan strode into view from behind a large black curtain and our applause reached a crescendo. He wore a red Olympic windbreaker with "Canada" emblazoned vertically on one forearm, a white dress shirt and black pants. He waved to the crowd as he walked along a red carpet. A TV cameraman a metre away backed up, capturing Dylan's entrance to this Olympic moment. Dylan veered left toward the podium, away from the camera operator, to accept his bronze medal for shot put, won during the 29th Olympic Summer Games in Beijing, China, August 15, 2008.

But we were not in Beijing and we were not cheering from the bleachers of China's Bird's Nest Stadium. The date was February 15, 2015—six and a half years after the 2008 Olympics. Coincidently, this presentation happened on the 50th anniversary of the adoption of Canada's new and distinctive red maple-leaf flag, now being waved in the hundreds by a forest of enthusiastic sports fans in the retractable, tiered benches and surrounding stadium seats of Kamloops' Tournament Capital Centre, the TCC, located on the southern boundary of Thompson Rivers University's campus. The TCC's Field House provided the venue for this sports event. The two-hundred-metre indoor track and the Centre's basketball and volleyball courts were blocked off by the tall screen in front of the main seats, where Dylan waited before his introduction. In the background, the city's annual Van Ryswyk indoor track meet provided an Olympic-like ambience in the official presentation area where Dylan would be honoured.

On his way to the podium, Dylan stopped in front of the stage to hug and thank his coach, Dr. Anatoliy Bondarchuk. He ran up onto the symbolic platform—the crowd boomed "Dylan! Dylan!" and to punctuate our enthusiasm, all one thousand or so of us jumped to a standing ovation, stomping our feet on the aluminum bleachers, creating quite a racket! The crowd buzzed, rejoicing for Dylan, a Kamloops kid who persevered to become an Olympian, a dream accomplished through hard work and dedication. For many of us, this might be as close to an official Olympic event as we would ever attend. We made the most of it—we were determined to replicate the one small isolated moment that had eluded him in Beijing years earlier on the world's stage.

Before Scott Russell called Dylan out, a slew of Canadian Olympians and visiting dignitaries filled the rows of the VIP seats on the floor directly in front of the stage. Media from around the world ringed the main area. While they set up, a trio of past champions—comprising Nancy Greene, a gold and silver Olympic medallist in skiing and current member of our Senate in Ottawa; Abby Hoffman, a former 800 metre track star; and Hayley Wickenheiser, four-time Olympic gold medallist in women's ice hockey—fluttered a full-sized

Canadian flag, holding it up to pose for a few pictures before they passed it on to Dylan's mom, Judy, to hold onto until the end of the proceedings.

When it was time to begin, Scott Russell took his place on the stage in front of four flags: two Canadian and two Olympic. He welcomed us and commenced the ceremony with a short biography of Dylan's Olympic quest and the reason for our gathering—the awarding of the Olympic bronze medal to Dylan for his 3ᵈ place finish in Beijing. Scott introduced the special guests, and one by one, politicians, Olympic and Canadian sports representatives praised Dylan for his accomplishment, and they acknowledged his fortitude during his Olympic journey culminating on that February day in his hometown, Kamloops.

On August 15, 2008 in Beijing, Andrei Mikhnevich of Belarus placed 3ᵈ in shot put, bumping Dylan's hurl of 21.04 metres off the podium—Dylan's throw missed the medal by a centimetre. On a massive TV screen above the TCC's stage, a slideshow ran throughout Dylan's official introduction. One photo in particular captured the twenty-seven-year-old, six-foot, four-inch, 340-pound Dylan sitting on a bench in Beijing with his head down—pushed physically to the limit of body and being. That was then: for this ceremony, he held his head high.

What changed things? The International Association of Athletics Federations confirmed Mikhnevich had tested positive for performance-enhancing drugs as early as 2005, so the International Olympic Committee disqualified his 2008 Beijing results and that elevated Dylan back to his rightful 3ᵈ place finish—entitling him

Ward Pycock

to the bronze medal. The Olympic Committee recovered the original medal and it was shipped to Kamloops for Dylan's official Olympic ceremony.

The big moment arrived. Scott introduced Hayley Wickenheiser. She walked over to Dylan, who waited atop the podium. She shook his hand. A young woman brought the medal over on a tray. The crowd fell solemnly silent. Dylan stooped down and Hayley stretched up to place the ribbon, with the medal dangling from it, over his head. She said something and made Dylan smile. She hugged him in congratulations and departed. He grinned and held the medal up in the fingers of his right hand for all the world to see, and simultaneously waved to all his fans joining him in Kamloops with his left hand—as if to say, See! Here it is! We responded with more deafening, metallic foot stomping and chants of "Dylan! Dylan!"

In a poignant moment, after Dylan acknowledged us, he took his first quick peek at his medal—yes, it was real; yes, it was the original; yes, it was vindication for being a clean athlete!

Next, Abby Hoffman approached the base of the podium. She shook his hand and they hugged. She attached Dylan's official Olympic pin to his sports jacket. Finally, a young local athlete presented him with a

85

replica bouquet of flowers, a copy of the one he would have received in Beijing. She shook his hand too, making the big man beam humbly.

Together, we sang *O Canada* enthusiastically, just like at any sports tournament. When our anthem ended, he jumped down to retrieve the flag, the one we saw earlier in the hands of the trio of Canadian women athletes, from his mother. He ran a victory lap, hoisting up the flag, much to the delight of the applauding fans.

Dylan skipped up the steps to the stage and delivered his speech.

"I'm happy to have it back in Canada, where it really belongs. It just shows if you listen to your coach and you're dedicated and you work hard, you can do it clean. I'm a prime example of that." Yes, he certainly became a champion for integrity and dedication—achieving his goals and doing it all drug free, relying on his physical and mental stamina. As well, he proved to be a testament to patience—waiting six and half years through the turmoil and repatriation drama to be awarded the Olympic medal he now held in his hand.

When he finished, the official dignitaries and presenters joined him onstage for photographs. Finally, Dylan entered the media scrum in front of a small Olympic Canada backboard. Following the interviews, he signed autographs graciously, including my Team Canada jersey, and posed for more photographs. The crowd thinned. The final photos of the day were snapped with his mother proudly at his side.

I didn't know at the time that Dylan was recovering from elbow surgery. After years of throwing the hammer and shot put, bone chips had impeded his ability to compete. Dylan retired from competition before the 2016 Summer Olympics held in Rio, and he shifted into coaching for the Kamloops Track and Field Club (https://kamtrack.ca). He works out of the TCC, teaching the upcoming generation the values he lived by and the importance of competing clean, a true, lasting legacy of his athletic career: certainly a cause worth supporting on that February day in 2015.

Ward attended UBC with a focus on creative writing and drama. Later, he earned a master's degree from UNBC in Prince George. He moved to Kamloops in 2003.

Ward has written a handful of family history books and memoirs, including *The House of Little Amanda: a personal adawx*, recounting his marriage to Maggie and the start of their family.

Ward joined the IAG in 2017. His novel the *Solstice Sphere* won the Dr. Robert and Elma Schemenauer award for a Kamloops themed work in 2018. He continues to write fiction full time and a bit of non-fiction.

WHO AM I
By Dana Ramstedt

Who am I
In this moment?
Not yesterday
Nor tomorrow.
Here, now, in this moment,
In this breath,
I am a farmer's partner,
His other half.
Not because I must,
Because I want to.
In this moment
I share in his joy
His love of providing,
Bringing rich green grass
To blossom, to rich round bales.

Four-wheel drive.
Hazards flashing,
Stay back, be aware of our load.
Our bounty takes the journey home.
To sustain our herd through winter
Until new growth springs forth.

In this moment,
I exist in this environ
Of security, knowing I am all he needs.
That we are one in our goals.
Amidst rain showers

Kamloops Tapestry

And lightning strikes,
I lend him my strength, my joy.

I bask in being loved,
In being respected for who I am,
Not for what I can give.
In this moment,
Secure behind the wheel,
I am content.

Dana Ramstedt

HAMMOCK AT SUNSET

By Dana Ramstedt
In the Hammock
Mid-August
Autumn on the wind
Tick Tick Tick
Irrigation heads
Count the seconds
Measure the days
Of Summer

Corn Tassels
Brown and dry
Promise cobs
Tasting of sunshine
Warm butter
Shining chins
Kernels squirt
Across the table

Heat of the day
Warms the fabric
Hammock chain
Creaks as I turn
To the fruit trees
Pears ripen
Young branches
Stretch skyward

"♪Day's done/

Kamloops Tapestry

Gone the sun....♪"
Drops behind the hills
Yellow to orange
To pink
Rays reach up
Gradient palette
Filters into the blue

Bats streak
Cry locating
Dusk meal
Owls hoot
Mice scurry
Sunset in the hammock
The Apex of my day

Dana Ramstedt

I GOT BLOCKS!

By Dana Ramstedt

Our adventure started out simple enough.

We signed the purchase agreement in July, and from that day on, every weekend until December first, we hauled the contents of our house and barn from Langley to the delightful community of Pritchard. A modest twenty-one acres with a 12 × 72–foot mobile home sitting smack dab in the middle of the site of our new home.

"I'm going to have to move the trailer to the gentle slope on the other side of the orchard." My hubby, Andy, decided. "Shouldn't take much to make it level. Look at the view we'll have," he said, sweeping in his arm in a wide arc.

Beyond the expanse of our lush green pastures was the Trans-Canada Highway, then a double set of train tracks and the South Thompson river forded by a one-lane wooden bridge. My eye continued across the fields and up the steep side of hills that looked as if a giant had cut their tops off with a butter knife. Those plateaus lent a unique perspective to the beauty stretching north toward Chase and south to Kamloops.

Okay, move the trailer and live in it until the house is built. Now that sounds easy, right? Of course not.

First step: find a heavy machine operator with the know-how to slide the square peg into the round hole, so to speak. His job would require him to tow the unwieldy mobile home to the end of the driveway, turn it at an 90-

degree angle and account for the slope that would leave the front end six feet lower than the end. He must also place it to run parallel with the fence line, and not run over the septic tank—that turned out to not be where we thought it was—all while we were off-site.

Have you ever been in a camper or trailer when it is being moved? Well, I have, and it gives precarious footing at best. Now, fill most of the cupboards, then set up the kitchen and the other rooms along the long, thin building.

"Aww, it'll be fine," Andy said, his expression making it clear he thought I was being over-dramatic when I tied the handles of the cupboards and duct-taped many of the drawers in an attempt to anchor everything in place. It all *was* fine until the gentle slope of the orchard turned out to be more of a hill.

We pulled into the driveway on the toasty August afternoon just as the mobile was set in place. She looked as if the merest of breezes—which are common in Pritchard—would send her careening down the hill and into the pasture.

Thankfully, my experience of being in a moving camper, had warned me to secure as much as possible, because when I peeked in through the windows of that crazily canted home, I saw the refrigerator waiting at the entrance to the living room. The metal trim holding the carpet down had stopped the harvest yellow fridge from having a chat with the TV under the far windows of the living room. In a mound of flour on the kitchen linoleum rested the shattered glass cover of the kitchen light.

Dana Ramstedt

Jack, the heavy machine operator, bless his soul, had laid all the chairs and lamps on their sides. He had also turned the kitchen table onto its top, and it had gaily sailed down the living room carpet and docked against the couch under the windows.

All the contents in the cupboards were straining at the ties. The cutlery drawers were trying to escape their moorings too. The bedroom dresser drawers *had* escaped and spilled my dainties all over the carpet. Even the shower curtain hung at a jaunty angle.

I was so glad to have the camper on our truck, because trying to sleep at such a crazy angle would have been fodder for some very strange dreams.

With the twisting and turning during her final move, the walls of the thirty-three-year-old lady had buckled, leaving all the wallpaper seams askew. I laughed in relief because it could easily be put to rights.

When Jack arrived early the next morning, Andy and the crew got to work levelling the mobile home. The living room end went up four feet, up five feet, and up and up, until finally, it was six feet off the ground. It balanced on temporary supports but there was no getting around it—our home had to be level!

We were allowed to go in and out through the kitchen door, only to midway down the trailer's length. Even so, I felt certain the whole precarious structure might tip over any minute, especially after one of the jacks slipped and the side nearest the apricot tree shuddered before the trailer settling back onto the support beams. No wild party at our house that night.

Kamloops Tapestry

At week's end we returned late in the day and gingerly unloaded more boxes. Early Saturday morning, the crew and machinery idled as they waited for the all-important delivery. The temperature climbed and tensions mounted.

I was sorting boxes when Andy clomped up the steps. He was as excited as a little kid with a new toy.

"I got blocks!" he yelled through the screen door. I put on my boots and, camera in hand, hurried outside. It was reassuring to see how conscientious the crew were to avoid damaging the apricot and nectarine trees that shaded their efforts.

Yes, indeed we had blocks: giant concrete interlocking, stackable blocks, the kind used as retaining walls along the highway. The sixteen-wheeler puffed and wheezed as it sat in the driveway. On the flat bed waited ten of the enormous blocks.

For the rest of that weekend, the reticulating dozer pushed, pulled and lifted those blocks until they were positioned under our home. All the way from the bedroom end to the four wide windows of the living room, the mobile was finally balanced and level. My footing was now secure as I watched the rest of the action from those same windows.

I remembered how easy it had sounded. "We'll set her in the orchard," Andy had said. "The apricot and peach tree will give us lots of shade, and the view will be spectacular!"

We lived in the mobile home for two years while we built our house. After which it took on the role as a rental for our farm workers, and later on as accommodation for my sister, Karen.

Pritchard has been our home for twelve years and the view is even more spectacular from the second-floor sundeck of our house. From our "view room," we look out over the Pritchard bridge and the South Thompson River. The Trans-Canada now runs four lanes of highway across a chunk of our once-pasture, and we can no longer see the train tracks. But even with all the changes in our lives, little compares to the excitement of that morning when…Andy got blocks!

Kamloops Tapestry

STRESSES EASE

By Dana Ramstedt

Ages older than forever
Here because of changing weather
Ice, snow, sun and time
All is as from this clime

Be as days or millennia
Two then one by Thera
Scripture, page, chapter, verse
Big Bang shook the universe

Close by air, hour, drive
Countless miles as we thrive
In a corner near the coast
Watched close by the heavenly Host

Change local, change a life
Man and woman, husband, wife
From there to here
Away from peers.

Lay foundation, raise a roof
Check my smile, see the proof
Mountains close, the river by
Move to Kamloops? I asked, "Why?"

Time goes fast, glaciers slow.
Yet years stretch, long to go.
Every day, I raise my eyes

Dana Ramstedt

To drink the vista I espy.

The constant wind blows cares away
This is the place I plan to stay
Nowhere have I felt such peace
Each day I greet, my stresses ease.

Breath deep, exhale slow
As journeys are, I've far to go
Summer sun, winter cold
My love for Kamloops'll never grow old.

Dana Ramstedt's writing career hit the ground running when she discovered the magic of a word processor. This tech allows her to tighten the weft and weave of her works.

Writing in 'most every genre, her prose and poetry have taken awards in such contests as the SIWC, Van. Story Slam, the Vancouver Sun and the Cecelia Lamont, and most recently the Schemenaur Awards. Her work is published in *Grainews, Manitoba Cooperator* and the *Rag*.

With the IAG, she held many positions as well as president. She worked on four of the six *Collected Works* editions. weavinwordsme2@gmail.com

Eileen Bell

FROM SELKIRK TO SAGEBRUSH

By Eileen Bell

CNR Train Station-Kamloops BC. September 1908

Passengers are scattered across the large room.

Near the top of the wall, a small window is open midway across the room. An afternoon breeze drifts lazily through the window, carrying with it, a whiff of warm late summer air and beyond a chilly stillness from the Thompson river. A pretty dark-haired girl in a bonnet, a long dress and thin coat sits alone on the bench by the far corner wall. She is reading a book and occasionally glances at her watch.

Henry, Arthur, and two other younger boys bustle through the swinging door of the station hauling their cases and bags. Arthur ducks his head through the doorway and then trips over his bag. Henry reaches out a hand to help but Arthur pushes him away. Henry steps back and laughs, brushing a thick lock of hair away from his forehead and grins slyly at his brother.

"Ur ye looking at that lass across the room then Arthur? Better watch where those feet are steppin' or the pretty lasses will nae be comin' your way."

"Ah-ah. Stop yer jaggering then. The door rise is ju- just too low for the likes a' me is a-all."

Fred chimes in. "He's got his knickers in a knot for the lassies alright."

Kamloops Tapestry

The other boys, Stewie and Fred, chortle. "That stutterin' will nae help 'im either."

"Ah. Shut yer gobs. Henry points toward the benches. What are you doing standin' around the door? Go park yerselves ye' willy nits."

The boys scramble over each other and their belongings in their haste to be the first to the long straight-backed bench in the middle of the room.

Henry stays by the door, peering through a nearby window. The light breeze from the high window wafts a slightly dank smell from the river. The mountains overhead are mostly treeless, but peaceful in their barrenness.

"I wonder what that yellow carpet-like stuff is, growing on the mountain's surface. Such a different countryside. I bet the summer sun can burn down from those bare mountains onto the town. Not much growin' in them hills tae absorb the heat. The wheat fields in the valley where we're goin' to work, must be basking in that heat and ripe for the harvest.

Mr. Holmes, emerges disheveled, from the steam train that has carried them from the coastal port of Vancouver. Passes through the door and walks by Henry without a glance sideways and hurries toward the scattered boys.

"Now my boys," he harps after them. "Slow down, slow down."

As he hurries along Mr. Holmes brushes absent crumbs from his shirt and runs his fingers through his hair.

Henry watches from beside the station entrance. *Holmes- He tries so hard at times to be in charge, but, ach, he's already making a muck of it.*

He sees Mr. Holmes raise his hands in the air; then falter like an absent-minded, orchestra conductor who's forgotten his tempo. Then Mr. Holmes recalls his instructions for the boys.

"We've a bit to wait, boys, for the train to Ashcroft. It's a short ride. and we shall be there before nightfall. We'll have to walk along from the station to the ranch, but we'll have time to set up out tents outside before dark. Take your seats and I shall purchase our tickets."

Arthur and the other boys sprawl across the bench. Henry comes and sits close beside Fred and pushes against his back and shoulders to force him to sit up.

The girl in the corner glances over at the unruly group, then looks away quickly.

"The wee lass is spottin' ye again Arthur," Fred smirks, looking straight ahead, as he grudgingly sits up.

He pushes against Henry's chest to shove him away. "Don't be sittin' on me ye hefty gruff. "

Fred pokes Arthur in the side with his elbow.

"She likes how you been so gracefully fallin' a' ower yer feet. Ye daft, clumsy oaf."

Kamloops Tapestry

"S'no Arthur who's getting her attention," Henry, raises his head to direct Fred's gaze across the room.

They all stare across the room. Mr. Holmes is chatting with the young woman and has her full attention.

Henry puts his hand to his lips to quiet the boys, so he can hear what Holmes and the girl are saying. He shakes his head mistrustingly.

Mr. Holmes walks slowly past the girl sitting on the bench. He looks towards her with a friendly nod and a smile. She looks up from her book.

"Mr. Holmes is it? May I talk with you a minute, Sir? You are from the borderlands in Scotland; you have travelled a long way. You and all your charges must be weary and needing a meal and a good night's rest."

Is he flirting with that young lass? Who is she tae him? Why doesn't he look after these lads as is his duty- his job- as their schoolmaster? Why am I always left seein' to these luddy louts? Is that why he was beggin' Arthur and me to come along on this trip? So I could do his job for him? On the train from Vancouver he sat up front and chatted on with the other passengers. He nae said a word to any of us the whole time and just now he come through the station door without even seein' I was there.

"I am here to welcome you to Kamloops and accompany you and your young men on the train to Aschcroft this evening," the young woman continues.

"Yes," Mr. Holmes answers, as he sits carefully beside her on the bench. "Ashcroft Manor? You must be the daughter of Jack Stillwater. Your father - does he own and operate the Inn as well as the Stillwater Ranch? Such a pretty young lady- May I ask your name?"

"Margaret, Margaret Stillwater. I have several older brothers and sisters. My sisters are married and are busy with their own families and my brothers are helping with ranch duties and operations, so I am left to manage the Inn. I do enjoy the day to day hustle and bustle and like to make my own decisions and as long as the Inn is profitable, I'll keep doing that."

"That's mighty fine, Miss Stillwater."

"With your permission, Mr. Holmes, I would like to give you and the boys dinner and a bed free of charge tonight at the Ashcroft Inn. This is my welcoming gift."

"I am most delighted with your offer. Why not call me Jack, Jack Holmes it is? He smiles as he reaches to shake her small, gloved hand. I shall inform the boys immediately. They will be so pleased not to have to spend their first night inland in a drafty tent."

Mr. Holmes laughs at his own weak attempt at humor, then a blush creeps across his face as Margaret fails to laugh. She nods and smiles politely.

Now, Henry sees Holmes, strutting along, excited with his own importance, hurrying towards the bench.

I dinae care if she has invited us tae spend the night at her Inn. He's a fool.

"Holmes be damned!" he spews for all in earshot.

He stands flush in Holmes' face to prevent him from taking a seat.

"What are you up tae Holmes?"

"Henry? Pardon me?" Holmes steps back.

Kamloops Tapestry

"Getting polite now ur ye? He jabs a finger into Holmes chest. Goin' tae sit with her on the train, aye? Yer so-oo polite when yer' gettin' up tae no good."

He waves his arms crazily in Mr. Holmes face. His words fly from his mouth, so quickly he hardly knows what's passing his lips.

Henry only half hears the boys snickering.

"I'm no goin' with ye tae the hay field or the Inn or whatever plans yer makin'."

"I was just about to say--"

"Dinae fret yerself"

Henry grabs his bag and tumbles through the swinging door. A few drops of rain pucker against his thin coat. He sinks down and crouches against the corner of the station wall.

"*What* am *I* goin' to do now?"

The raindrops splash off his hardened leather boots. Henry rubs his face and smacks his fist against his forehead. The rain falls harder now soaking through his pant legs. He looks up from his soggy outpost. Raindrops slide along to the end of the overhang and down to the ground. As he steps out, rain splatters down his neck. He reaches to wipe away the water and then backs into the flank of a large stallion tied to a hitching post, in front of the station. The horse snorts and raises his front legs and then his back haunches in the air. Henry grabs the bridle and pulls down on it to try to settle him, but the stallion raises upper body and snorts once again, shaking his head and mane. Henry speaks softly to the horse, while pulling down on the bridle once more.

"Settle me lad. Yer doin' fine. Just me's the clumsy fellow."

Henry steps back, but too late, as the horse comes down, with his front left hoof onto Henry's right foot. Henry backs away and stumbles across the train yard, up the slight hill and onto a wide street.

Nothing's goin' right today. The damn horse, he's got it in for me too.

The signpost reads Lorne Street. Lining the street are several tarpaper shacks and two sturdier looking wooden buildings with fenced yards behind, which housed assorted animals. There were fields of stubby grass and sagebrush in between. He walks with his head down, his shoulders hunched against the rain, dragging his injured foot behind. A donkey brays from someone's backyard as he walks by. The bray makes him startle and jerk his head up. He sees a bench ahead, limps over and sits heavily, loosening his boot, he examines his injury. He removes his one bloody sock. It is cut, bruised and beginning to swell, but he sees no bones out of place. He puts his foot back in his sock and eases his boot back on. He ties his lace loosely. A rooster crows in the distance. Sitting on the bench, he remembers the last conversation he and Arthur had with their Father, who was a respected, Anglican Minister for Selkirk and the surrounding area. Henry had wanted his father to understand why he and Arthur wished to take this trip to Canada. The conversation didn't go well.

***

Henry clears his throat and looks directly at his father- Charles, trying to quell his rising anxiety.

"We know ye been thinkin' and wantin' to ask about our plans, now we have our school- leaving papers. We'll here it is: We're plannin' to go along with Mr. Holmes, the schoolmaster and two school-boys to help with the September hayin' in a place called Ashcroft in BC.'s interior. As you ken, I like the outdoor work and Arthur- Arthur can speak for himself."

Henry could see now from this rain-soaked bench in this dusty, small town far across the ocean, how things had begun to go wrong. Arthur never did speak up much for himself. At least not in a manner that convinced Father to let them have their way. Arthur just spoke, not thinking about how Father or anyone else would react.

"What the devil. Ur ye mad boys? Canada - BC.?"

Arthur looked eagerly at Henry. His admiring expression says he is very sure Henry can persuade their father to allow them to travel on this month- long, haying trip.

"Nothin' but wild Indians ready with their hatchets or bow and arrows, ready tae scalp the white man. Good Lord! They attack trains. Did ye ever hear the story? What was his name? Bill Miner, but he was a white man from the United States, mind you. Near a place called Kamloops. Something like that. Jumps off a bluff overlooking the track onto the roof of the train and down into the car with his guns out ready tae shoot if the passengers don't give him everything they have. I heard he took all their shoes in one passenger car. And then leaving every decent, white passenger shoeless, he gave all the footwear-- he gave all white people's shoes to a tribe of Indians. What would they want with lady's heels? Aye, they caught him though. Nasty fellow- by all accounts. There are, of course, decent and hardworking ranchers and cowboys. Been readin' some books about the goings on in Canada. Very uncivilised. I forbid it. Ye will not go. Much too dangerous. And Arthur – Arthur-- Ye see what I'm sayin' of course, don't ye?"

Arthur gazes beseechingly at Henry, then back to his father.

"I-I want to go Father. N-no reason not to. We'll be looked after with Mr. Holmes k- keeping an eye out for us all. It's an adventure you see. And m-mum, she'll have less meals to get and cleaning to do with us gone for a month or so."

"Mother? What do' she have to do with this? Too tied to her apron strings, Arthur. Spending time helpin' your mother in the kitchen. Never seen the like. A big gaffer like you gettin' tangled in your wee mum's skirts."

"I like to help mum,"

Charles ignores Arthur, clears his throat, and looks again at Henry.

"You two ought to be doing men's work, but not way off in the wilds of Canada."

"Aw--h, Father you got your head stuck inside too many books," Henry chokes back the acid in his throat. He sits up straight in his chair. "'Tis no like it says in them books. We need to find out fer urselves."

Henry sees now, from his solitary bench on the side of a dirt road in a dusty town far from home, how things had gone wrong. Mr. Holmes had met the boys in the street the next day. He eagerly asked how it went with getting their father's permission to get on the boat to Canada.

"Nae sae good,"

"I'll get you two on that ship from Newcastle. I have your passports. Leaving tomorrow at 9 pm. Meet me here at 10:00 am. I'll be coming with the other boys and a horse and cart. We'll be in Newcastle by nightfall. Bring a wee bit of supper and whatever money you have." He patted Henry on the shoulder, then walked away.

Arthur cracks his knuckles, then runs his hands through his thick, curly red hair.

"It's n-not okay is it? Do you really think we can persuade father by tomorrow, Henry?"

"Leave it tae me. I'll get us sorted. We'll meet him tomorrow and be on the boat. "

***

I sorted it alright. I took Mum's pound notes she had stashed in the kitchen jar. Stealin' from ma ain mum. How low is that? Us sneaking out early next day before they were wakin'. Sittin' in the cafe the next morning with Arthur, looking out for Holmes and his lads. Arthur asked me why we were leaving for Canada without a real goodbye. Easy tae lie to Arthur. I told him I'd said goodbye for us both the night before. So, here we are. I need tae go back and get the train. Can't leave him alone. I really can't trust Holmes.

The rain has stopped. He tries to walk on the higher ground between the wagon-ruts, but it is slow going with his injured foot. Blood oozes between his toes. The sun is setting across the river and scattering flickers of light across the road. He sees a few seagulls prancing along the shore looking for grubs and a white heron standing on a log out in the river, patiently waiting for his dinner. Henry drags himself through the wet dirt and gravel and across the rise to the station.

A train is pulling away. The train belches and hisses as it begins its short journey westward. Clouds of steam obliterates the scene around it. For a few moments Henry is mesmerized by the pulsating dampness of the disappearing train cars.

Damn the likes of it. They're goin' off without me. I've made a right mess now.

Inside the station Arthur is pacing the floor by the wicket. He cracks his knuckles and looks anxiously towards the door, then sees Henry come through the door and breaks into a wide grin.

"I saved ma t-ticket and I got your ticket from Mr. Holmes. Knew you'd be back. The Station Master says we can get a train to Ashcroft here in the mornin' He gave me a b-beer."

Henry grabs him in a bear hug and tries lifting him from the ground. He groans with pain and puts Arthur down quickly. "I am glad you waited."

Arthur looks down at his brother's foot. "Wha- goin' on with you? Yer limpin.'"

"Had a run in with a horse tied up outside. He got excited and came down a wee bit hard. Be better tomorrow," he said, lightly laughing.

"Ye have nothin' broke?"

"Nah," he says but winces in pain.

"Holmes was mad, but I told him. I told him I had to wait for ye. Ue you pleased with me?"

Kamloops Tapestry

"I'm pleased with you Arthur, but not with meself. I'm such a damn, daft fool for running off and now this," he says as he points to his foot.

"Ah need to learn tae wind in my temper."

"A daft fool." Arthur scoffs and punches Henry in the shoulder. "B-but-- We can sleep in the back room, the Station Master told me. Train leaves at 8 am. We're not sae bad off now, aye? But how will we get to the ra-ranch from the train in the mornin? With yer limpin' foot and all- that'll be a long stretch."

Arthur leads the way to the back room.

"I'll sort it. Never ye mind. I'll sort it."

Eileen Bell

Eileen lives in Kamloops, BC. She became interested in writing poetry and short stories while taking creative writing courses at the University of Waterloo in the 1990s. She has had poetry and short stories published in various anthologys and collections. Recently she has published an illustrated children's adventure/ fantasy book. She writes and performs in skits for local community groups.

WHERE AM I?

By Jan Petrar

Guess where in Kamloops the place I'm describing is... Answers at the end (no peeking!)

Place A

It's just past dawn and I am out before the crushing heat of the day. Parking my car on the edge of the turn-out, I step to the centre of the asphalt semi-circle. I gaze from this high viewpoint northward, my eyes taking in the breath-taking vista. The sun is rising to my right, the rivers and city lie ahead and downward as I position myself in this little-known place in the suburb with the prickly name on a street meaning the opposite of Low Prairie Place.

A breeze blows lightly. The valley below is backdropped by Mt. Peter and Paul. Quiet. I can see traffic lines snaking in the distance, but I am far from the noise and bustle. The birds are busy and bursting with sounds from melodic to croaky. I still my mind and slowly my body starts to move. It is my favourite place to do Tai Chi.

Place B

Heading east on the Trans-Canada, I exit, briefly skirt the edge of a round-about, and then head up the mountain. Winding my way up, the road then angles eastward. I stop and pause at my destination. My kids are now in their 30s, but years (nay... Decades!) ago, they marched here like little soldiers for ten months of the year. Little seems to have changed. I gaze at what must be one of the most spectacular playground views in the area, alive with kids wearing fashion-statement backpacks, jostling, running, laughing, kicking balls. There's one lonely little girl shuffling, looking downward like she's afraid to offend. She looks like she needs a friend. Yes, much has changed, but much remains the same.

Place C

Number 3 to Westsyde... Number 2 to Brocklehurst via Parkcrest... 16 to Juniper Ridge. Folks seek a place in the shade while waiting patiently for the machine bearing the orange LED sign that promises to take them to their destination. Skateboarders meander the area. Many of those waiting are smoking. Almost all are gazing at their phones as they wait, faces neutral. The hiss of air brakes releasing, of doors opening and closing. Converge, then disburse. A system of connections.

Place D

They say that those who live in the mountains are of two minds: there are those who like to live high and look down, and those who settle in the valleys and prefer to gaze upward. I started as the former, but now choose the latter. Getting less snow and fog and easier driving and walking are factors. This morning, in the early summer sunshine, I ventured up. I was in search of the highest dwelling within the city limits. I might be wrong, but I think it might be at the end of a winding, upward artery that snakes its way through the Aberdeen suburbs and bears the name of our closest ocean. I got to the top and found a little path with a few sturdy hikers basking in the stunning view. Later I checked the elevations online (who knew you could do that?) and I am probably right. I was at 890 metres. I live downtown at 366 metres, and often wander down to the shoreline at Riverside Park near the Rotary Bandshell (345 metres). Kamloops has its ups and downs.

Place E

I'm a prairie girl by birth and so my life was largely uncluttered by complex road navigation. For the most part, city streets met at right angles, and in the rural areas, often the only curves were the north/south correction lines which periodically adjusted the road system to compensate for the earth's curvature.

And then I moved to Kamloops. Yikes! I had to throw all that tidy organization out the window and instead deal with winding arterial roads. Saying "go north two blocks, then turn west for six blocks, then north again for two blocks and you're there," a common phraseology on the prairies, often became meaningless in my new mountain home. I eventually got used to not having a constant sense of precise direction, and instead learned to instead develop a broad, innate sense of where the Pacific Ocean was, establishing an anchor to the west. I'd often supplement my directional sense by tracking that big fiery ball in the sky.

But mountain geography doesn't explain the following really weird intersection. Why Oh Why does this street, a main thoroughfare I might add found in a completely flat area of the city, come to a set of lights and then take a 90 degree (well, close to 90) turn, yet retain its name? I cannot think of another place where I've seen this. Streets change name as they proceed in some cities (London is notorious for this... most streets change their name every few blocks!)

But who ever heard of a street that has one name travelling northward, and then the same street turns left at a right angle and continues westward? Or to put it another way (literally), this place has a name travelling eastward, and then retains the same name when you turn right 90 degrees and venture south? Or, put yet *another* way, no matter which of the four ways you approach this intersection, if you proceed straight ahead, the street name will have changed. I suspect for tourists and newcomers to the city, much flapping of maps and heated discussion between driver and navigator occurs. Even my phone's Siri seems a bit confused!

Place F

Let's pretend you're from the prairies passing through Kamloops on your way to Vancouver. You ask a local the name of the appropriate highway. They are likely to suggest "The _____". Sounds easy enough, so you continue on the freeway, searching for a sign that says "The _____ Highway".

Seeing no such sign, you now start to panic. You resort to thinking about the direction. Quick! What direction is it from Kamloops to Vancouver? West... or southwest you might think. According to our BC highway system, you're wrong. It's South. Kamloops to Vancouver is south. Really?

Still seeing no _____ sign, you conclude logically that it must be Highway #1. Right? Wrong. It's 5. But apparently the Department of Highways is short on numbers, so we have 5 or 5A. I love this clever sign pictured to the right. If you've figured out that Vancouver is "south", now which do you pick? 5 or 5A? There is a BIG difference so choose wisely.

Continuing to drive, the elevation begins to climb, as does the speed limit. You are now whizzing along at 120 clicks. You spot a highway sign sub-titled "The Yellowhead." Well, certainly *that* isn't your sought after "_____", right?

You pull over and take out a map. Examining the map options closely between Kamloops and Vancouver, you see a highway labelled "The _____", but you do not see one labelled The Yellowhead on your map. What is going on?

Let me review. The main highway between Kamloops and Vancouver is not Number 1, as logic would tell you, but rather Number 5. But be careful. There is a 5 and a 5A and they are vastly different. The signs note that one is referred to as The Yellowhead. But the locals and the maps say "The _____". You're taking a southbound route to go west.

I love my mountain home, but as for finding my way around? Sometimes I long for the simplicity of the prairies.

119

Kamloops Tapestry

Answers:

Vehicle pullout on High Forest Place in Rose Hill
Robert L. Clemitson Elementary School in Barnhartvale
Lansdowne Transit Exchange
Top of Pacific Way
The intersection of Tranquille Road, Fortune Drive and 8th Street
The highway/freeway from Valleyview heading up the mountain in the direction of Vancouver searching for a sign, *any* sign, that says "Coquihalla Highway"

NOTE: This is a repeat of the 180 degree rotated text just in case you are unable to use the Text Box rotated format.

Overlooking Cape Town (tripod photo by Jan Petrar)

Born in Regina, Jan has been a resident of Kamloops for 3 decades. Following careers in the travel industry and at Thompson Rivers University, she is now retired.

She has held community leadership roles:
PROBUS Club of Kamloops
Kamloops Symphony Orchestra

Multiple Sclerosis Society Kamloops Chapter
Rotary Club of Kamloops
She serves as a Board Member for:
Kamloops Adult Learners Society
Thompson Valley Orchestra

Interests include travel, music, Tai Chi, yoga, and lifelong learning. She has also written two books, *Travel, Turbulence and Technology* and *Around the World in 111 Days*, available at Chapters Kamloops or Amazon.

THE INTERIOR AUTHORS GROUP

We're a great bunch of people who just love to write, in all styles, forms, and genres. Maybe you've seen folks in Kamloops coffee shops dive into their bags for their electronic devices to tap out a few sentences, because to lose the great wording that's running through their brains would be a tragedy. Those folks may be members of the Kamloops-based Interior Authors Group. If not, maybe they should be!

What do we do? We meet monthly to support and lift each and to learn and grow in the craft of writing together. There is a workshop at each monthly meeting and guest speakers will come and knock our socks off every now and again too. Meetings at the North Shore Community Centre are also a place to come and read and discuss your work for feedback. It's such a boost talking about your current project with other fellow writers.

We're poets, we're song writers, we're bloggers, we're screenplay creators, we're literary authors, romance authors, mystery authors and every other genre and sub-genre you can come up with. We've got some truly talented non-fiction writers, and even a few journal writers have been known to be at a meeting or two. We're veteran authors, debut authors and a whole bunch of people who aspire to get that first book into print.

So if you want to learn more about the craft of writing, or about publishing and self-publishing, or if you want to rub shoulders with veteran authors who've made careers out of their skills with words, or even if you just want to improve your own story telling, come check us out!

www.ingramcontent.com/pod-product-compliance
Lightning Source LLC
Chambersburg PA
CBHW071247070526
44583CB00017B/2366